Elementary Music Rudiments

Mark Sarnecki

Intermediate

Elementary Music Rudiments© 2023 by San Marco Publications. All rights reserved.

All right reserved. No part of this book may be reproduced in any form or by electronic or mechanical means including Information storage and retrieval systems without permission in writing from the author.

ISBN: 9781896499093

Contents

Basic Rudiments Review	3
Accidentals	9
Major Scales	11
Minor Scales	18
Chromatic Scales	25
Whole Tone Scales	29
The Blues Scale	31
Pentatonic Scales	33
The Octatonic Scale	35
Identifying Scales	37
Intervals	39
Review One	50
Time	53
Review Two	70
Chords	73
Cadences	88
Review Three	95
Transposition	98
Review Four	103
Music Analysis	106
Practice Test	110
Terms and Signs	115
History Appendix	117

Basic Rudiments Review

Scales

The Major Scale

In a major scale, half steps occur between scale degrees $\hat{3}$ and $\hat{4}$, and $\hat{7}$ and $\hat{8}$ ($\hat{1}$).

The Natural Minor Scale

In a natural minor scale, half steps occur between scale degrees $\hat{2}$ and $\hat{3}$, and $\hat{5}$ and $\hat{6}$.

The Harmonic Minor Scale

In a harmonic minor scale, half steps occur between scale degrees $\hat{2}$ and $\hat{3}$, $\hat{5}$ and $\hat{6}$, and $\hat{7}$ and $\hat{8}$ ($\hat{1}$).

The Melodic Minor Scale

In a melodic minor scale, half steps occur between scale degrees $\hat{2}$ and $\hat{3}$, and $\hat{7}$ and $\hat{8}$ ($\hat{1}$) ascending; and between scale degrees $\hat{6}$ and $\hat{5}$, and $\hat{3}$ and $\hat{2}$ descending.

Key Signatures

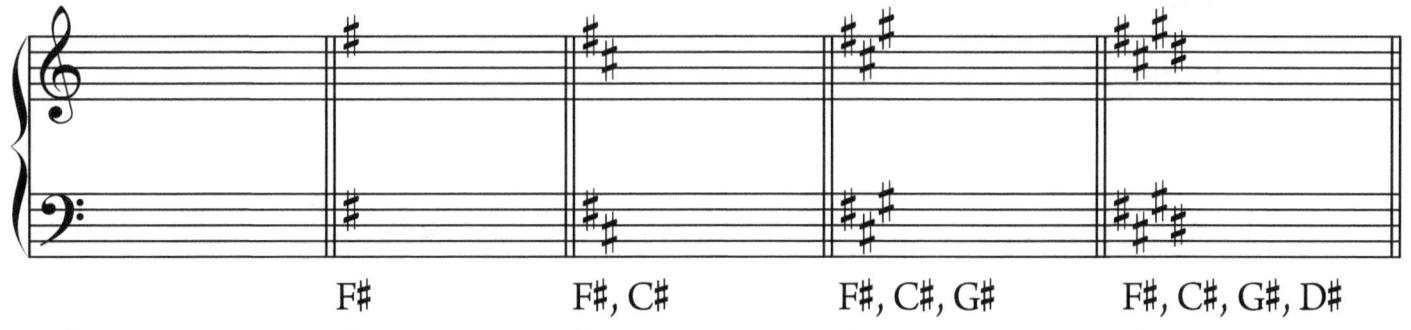

| C major | G major | D major | A major | E major |
| A minor | E minor | B minor | F# minor | C# minor |

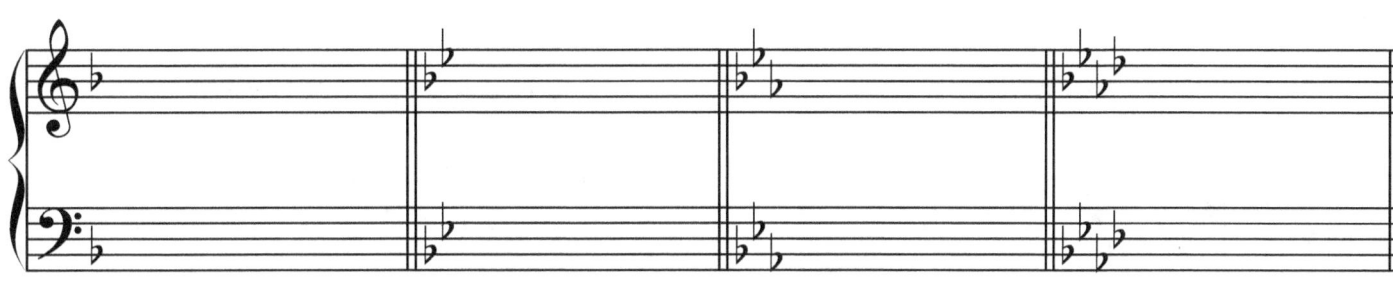

| F major | Bb major | Eb major | Ab major |
| D minor | G minor | C minor | F minor |

Intervals

per 1   maj 2   min 2   maj 3   min 3   per 4   per 5   maj 6   min 6   maj 7   min 7   per 8

Degrees of the Scale

$\hat{1}$ Tonic
$\hat{4}$ Subdominant
$\hat{5}$ Dominant
$\hat{7}$ Leading tone
$\hat{7}$ Subtonic (when $\hat{7}$ is not raised in the natural and melodic minor scale)

Triads

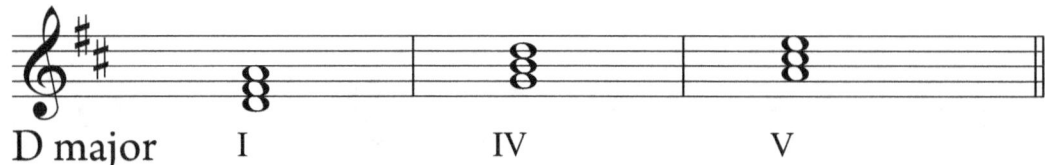

D major — I   IV   V

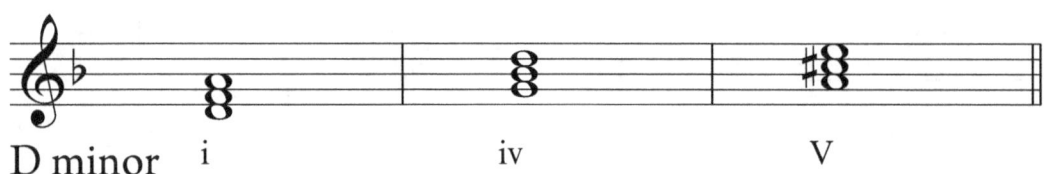

D minor — i   iv   V

Simple Time

Basic Rudiments Terms and Signs

a tempo	return to the previous tempo
adagio	a slow tempo (between *andante* and *largo*)
allegretto	fairly fast (a little slower than *allegro*)
allegro	fast
andante	moderately slow; at a walking pace
andantino	a little faster than *andante*
cantabile	in a singing style
con pedale, con ped.	with pedal
crescendo, cresc.	becoming louder
da capo, D.C.	from the beginning
da capo al fine, D.C. al fine	repeat from the beginning and end at *fine*
dal segno, D.S. al 𝄋	from the sign
decrescendo, decresc.	becoming softer
diminuendo, dim.	becoming softer
dolce	sweet, gentle
fermata ⌒	pause; hold note or rest longer than written value
fine	the end
forte, **f**	loud
fortissimo, **ff**	very loud
grazioso	graceful
larghetto	not as slow as *largo*
largo	very slow and broad
legato	smooth
lento	slow
maestoso	majestic
mano destra, M.D.	right hand
mano sinistra, M.S.	left hand
marcato, marc.	marked or stressed
mezzo forte, **mf**	moderately loud
mezzo piano, **mp**	moderately soft
moderato	at a moderate tempo

ottava, 8va	the interval of an octave
pedale, ped.	pedal
pianissimo, **pp**	very soft
piano, **p**	soft
prestissimo	as fast as possible
presto	very fast
rallentando. rall.	slowing down
ritardando, rit.	slowing down gradually
staccato	sharply detached
tempo	speed at which music is performed
tempo primo, Tempo I	return to the original tempo
tenuto	held, sustained

Signs

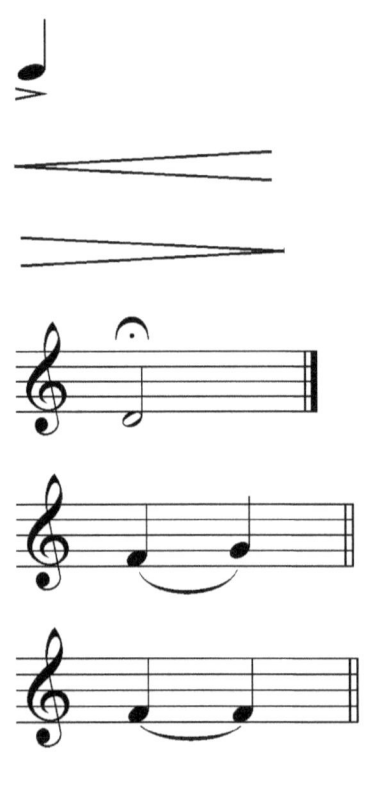

accent - a stressed note

crescendo - becoming louder

decrescendo - becoming softer

fermata - hold note or rest longer than written value

slur - play the notes smoothly (legato)

tie - hold for the combined value of the tied notes

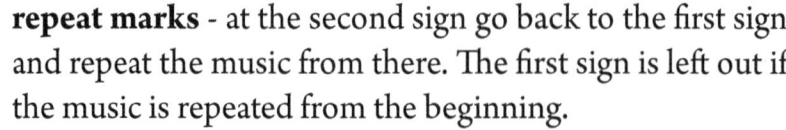

repeat marks - at the second sign go back to the first sign and repeat the music from there. The first sign is left out if the music is repeated from the beginning.

 **8va** - play one octave higher than written pitch.

 **8va** - play one octave lower than written pitch.

 **pedal symbol** - press/release the right pedal.

 staccato - play short and detached

 dal segno, D.S. - from the sign.

ACCIDENTALS

𝄪   The double sharp sign raises a natural note one whole step (two half steps), or raises a note that is sharp one half step.

𝄫   The double flat lowers a natural note one whole step (two half steps), or lowers a flattened note one half step.

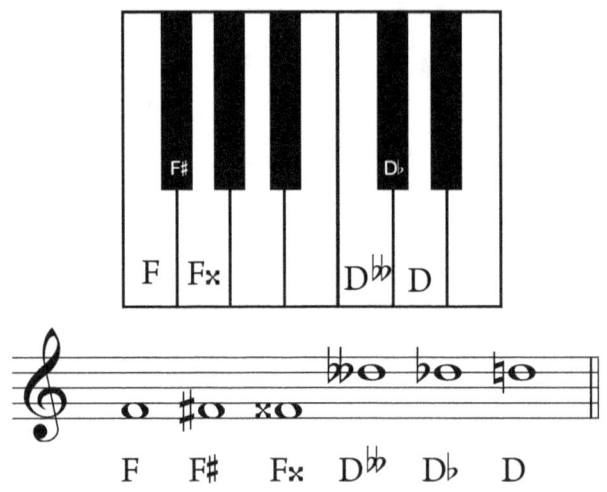

Every note, with the exception of G sharp/A flat, can have three names.

A half step that consists of two notes with the same letter name is called a *chromatic half step*.

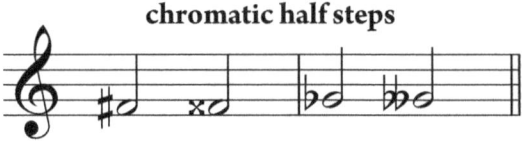

A half step that consists of two notes with different letter names is called a *diatonic half step*.

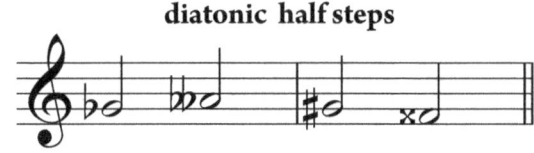

A *whole step* is made up of two half steps. Whole steps usually have two different letter names in alphabetical order. For example, C to D, A flat to B flat, and F double sharp to G double sharp are all whole steps.

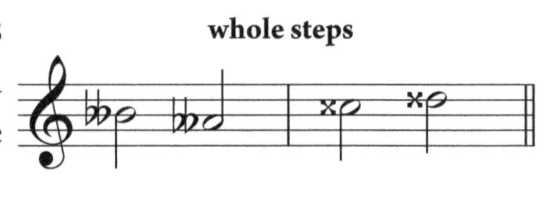

1. Write chromatic half steps above the following notes.

2. Write diatonic half steps above the following notes.

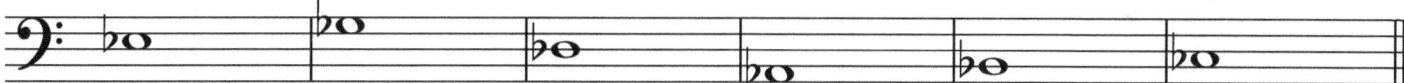

3. Write whole steps above the following notes.

4. Write chromatic half steps below the following notes

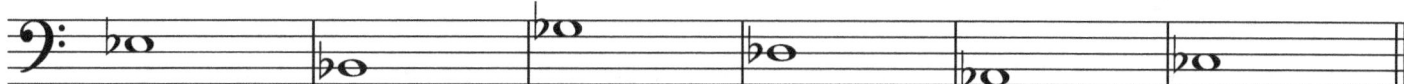

5. Write diatonic half steps below the following notes.

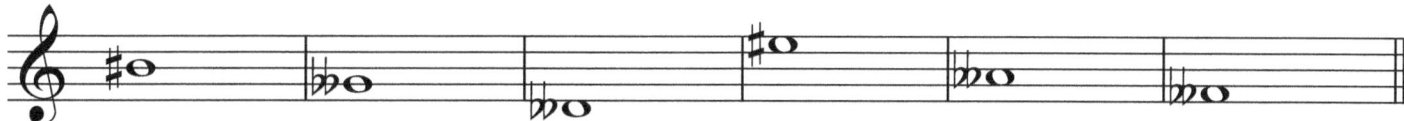

6. Write whole steps below the following notes.

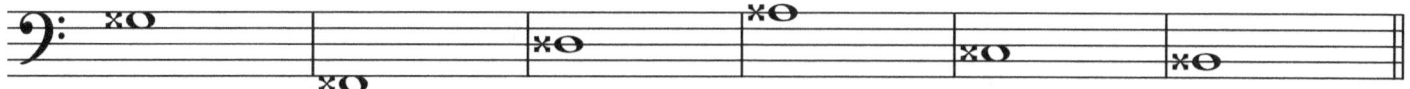

Degrees of the Scale

Every note or degree of a scale has a specific title. Here is a list of the names for the degrees of the scale:

$\hat{1}$ Tonic
$\hat{2}$ Supertonic
$\hat{3}$ Mediant
$\hat{4}$ Subdominant
$\hat{5}$ Dominant
$\hat{6}$ Submediant
$\hat{7}$ Leading tone

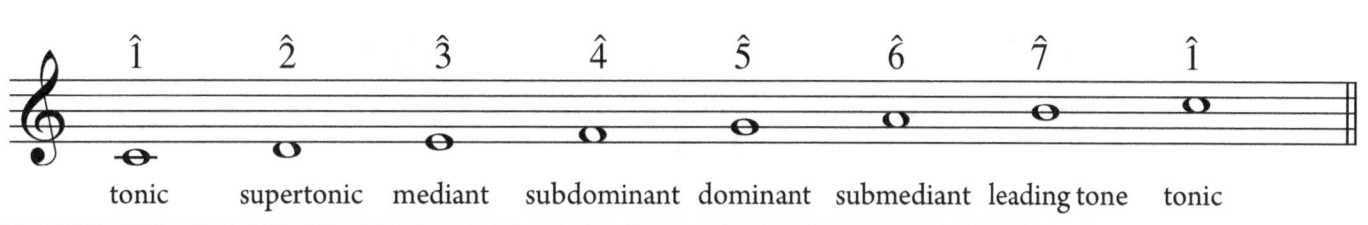

Major Scales

The Circle of Fifths

The circle of fifths relates keys by 5ths. We start with a circle divided into twelve sections, like a clock with C in the "12" position.

The sharp keys are set to the right (moving clockwise) in order of the number of sharps in their key signatures.

The flat keys are set to the left (moving counterclockwise) in order of the number of flats in their key signatures.

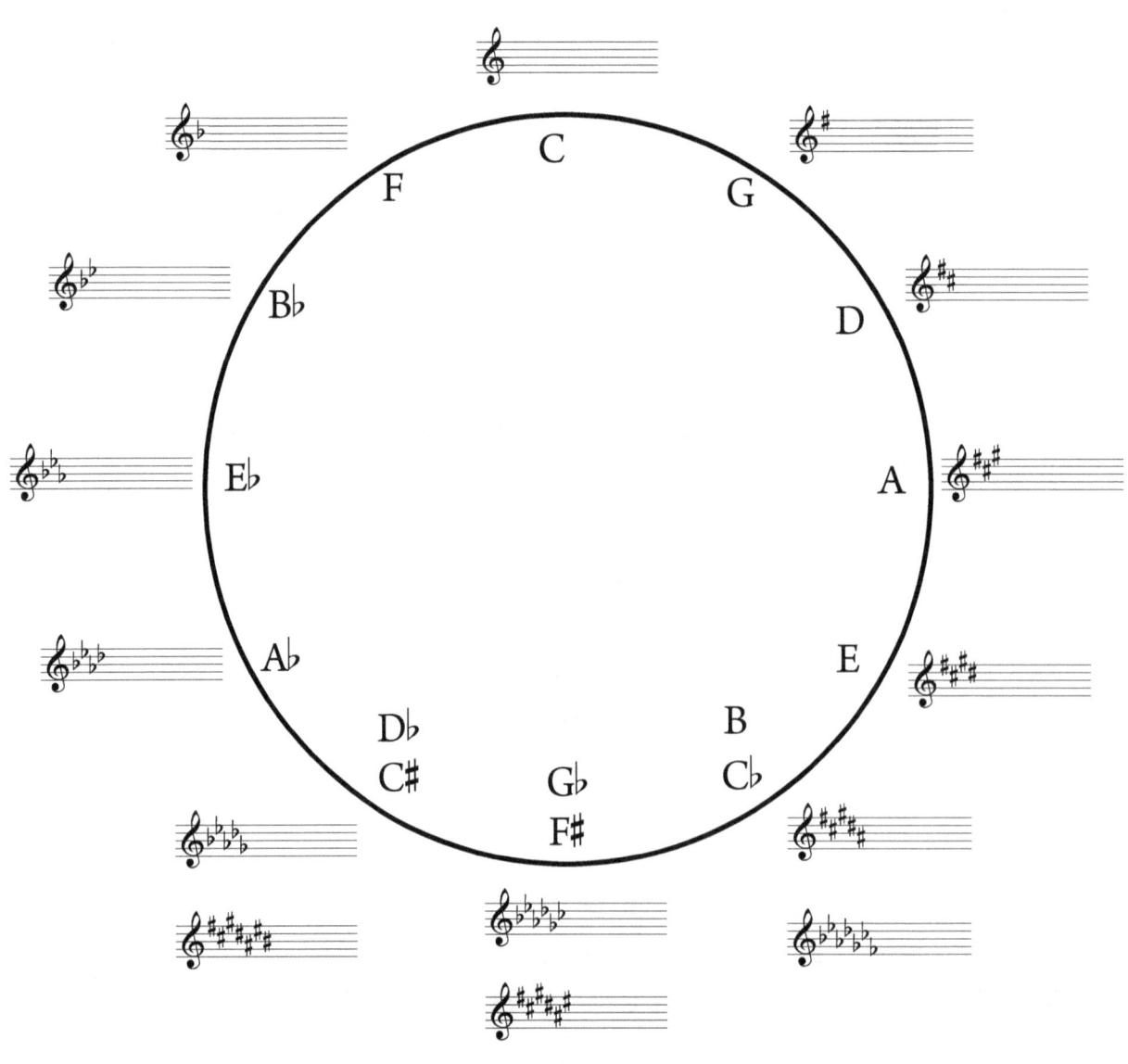

The arrangement of keys in the circle of fifths shows two things:

1. The distance between each key and the next is a 5th.
2. Three pairs of keys share the same spots on the circle:

    D flat/C sharp, G flat/F sharp, and C flat/B.

    These three pairs of keys are called **enharmonic**. They have the same pitch but the notes are named differently.

Here is the order of sharps as they appear in a key signature : F C G D A E B

Here is he order of flats as they appear in a key signature: B E A D G C F

Sharps and flats are grouped in a specific order when they are placed on the staff.
The following exercise shows the order of sharps as they appear on the staff.

1. Name the major key and write the sharps represented by each key signature below.

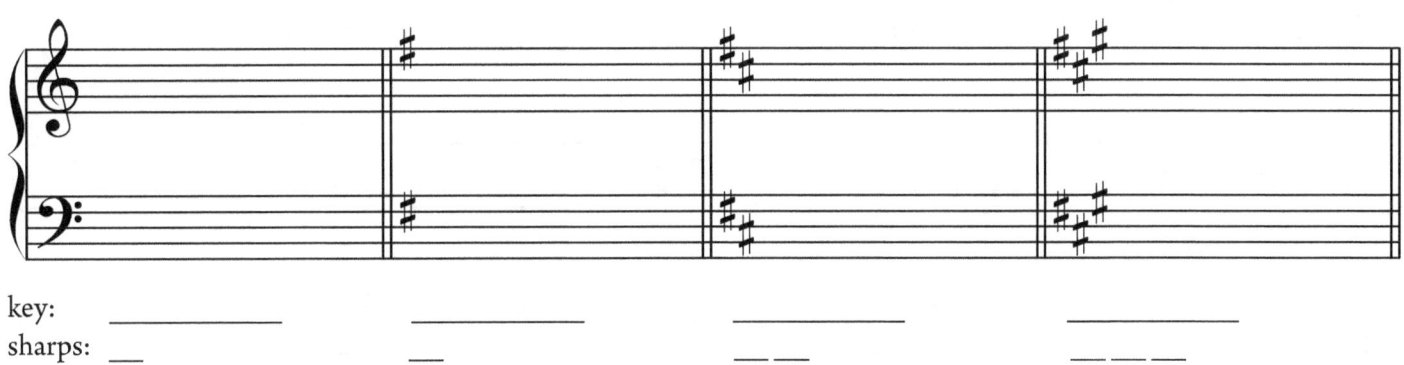

key: _____   _____   _____   _____
sharps: __   __   __ __   __ __ __

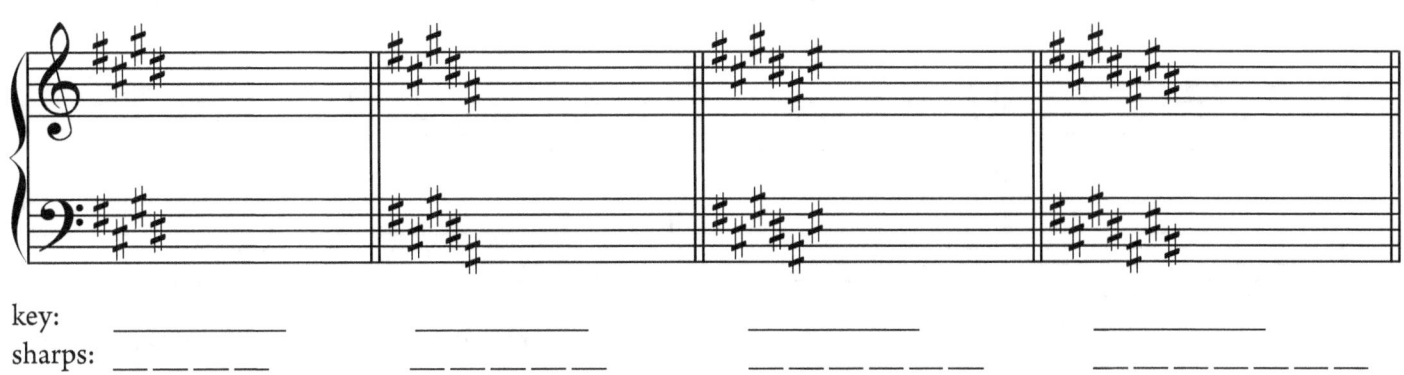

key: _____   _____   _____   _____
sharps: __ __ __ __   __ __ __ __ __   __ __ __ __ __ __ __ __ __ __ __ __ __

12

The following exercise shows the order of flats as they appear on the staff.

2. Name the major key and write the flats represented by each key signature below.

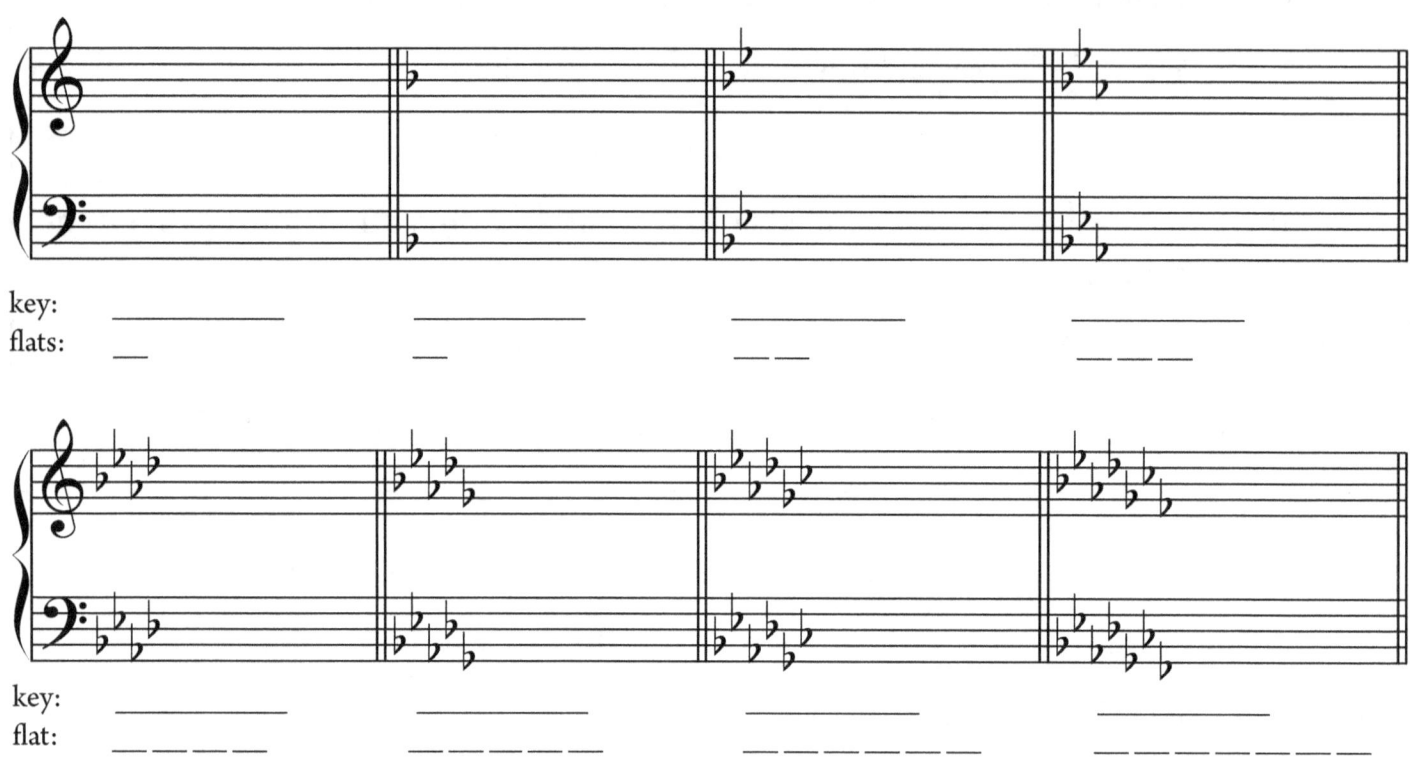

key: _____ _____ _____ _____
flats: __ __ __ __ __ __ __

key: _____ _____ _____ _____
flat: __ __ __ __ __ __ __ __ __ __ __ __ __ __ __ __ __ __ __ __ __ __

3. Write the following notes and key signatures on the grand staves below.

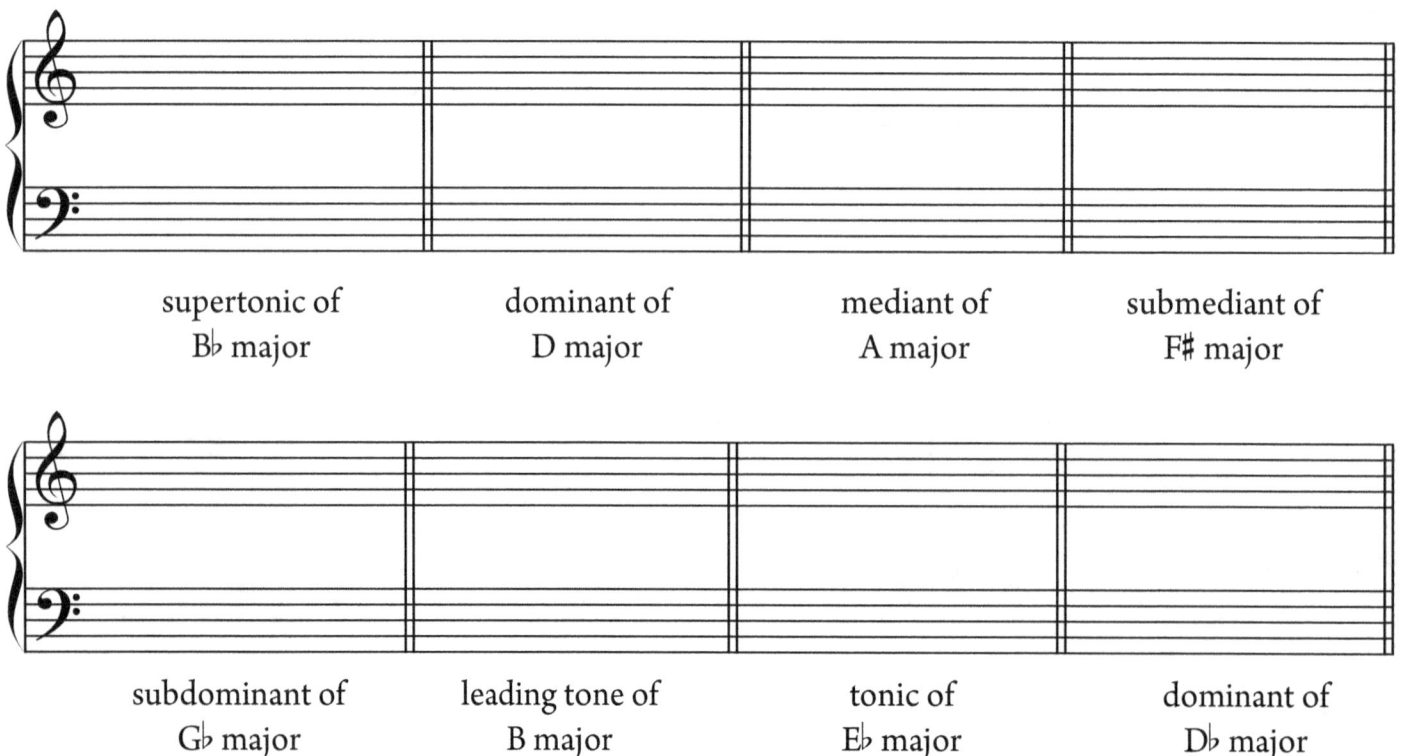

supertonic of   dominant of   mediant of   submediant of
B♭ major   D major   A major   F♯ major

subdominant of   leading tone of   tonic of   dominant of
G♭ major   B major   E♭ major   D♭ major

Here is the order of whole steps and half steps in a major scale.

whole - whole - half - whole - whole - whole - half

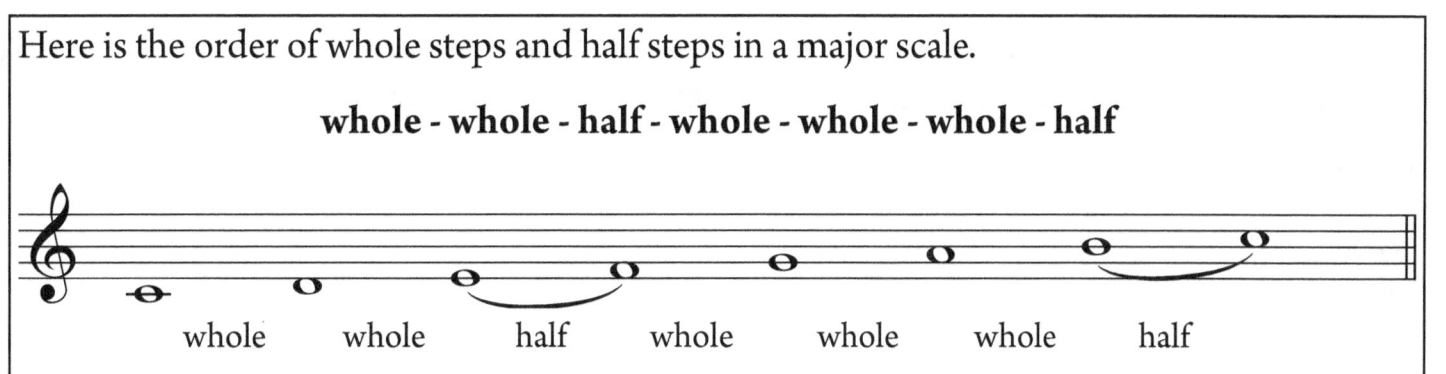

1. Write the following scales in half notes, ascending and descending, using key signatures. Mark the half steps with a slur.

B major

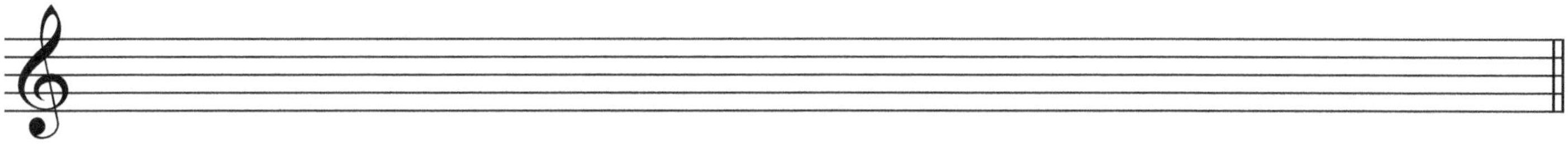

E♭ major

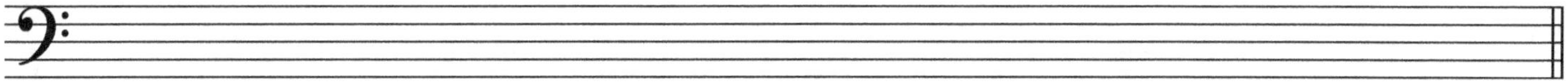

F♯ major

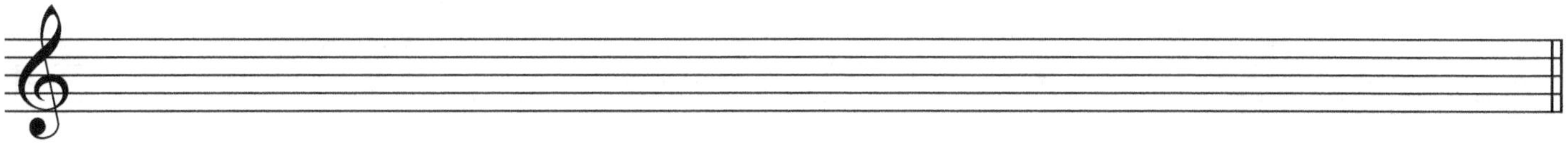

A♭ major

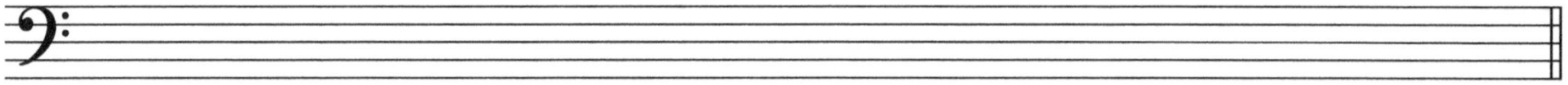

E major

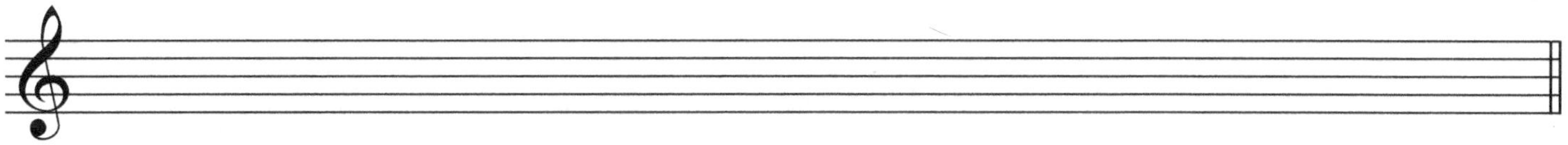

G major

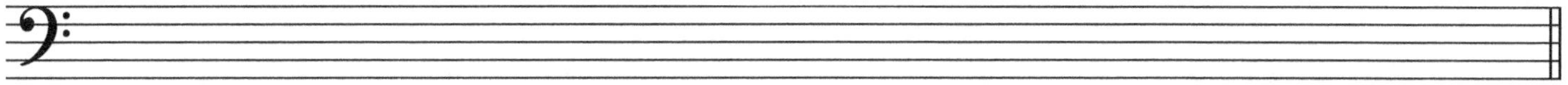

2. Write the following scales in quarter notes, ascending and descending, using accidentals instead of a key signature. Mark the dominant notes (D) and leading tones (LT).

B♭ major

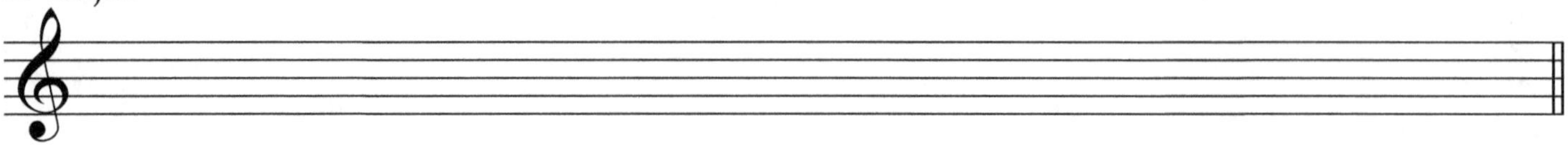

F major

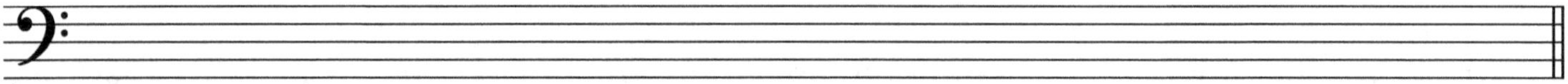

F♯ major

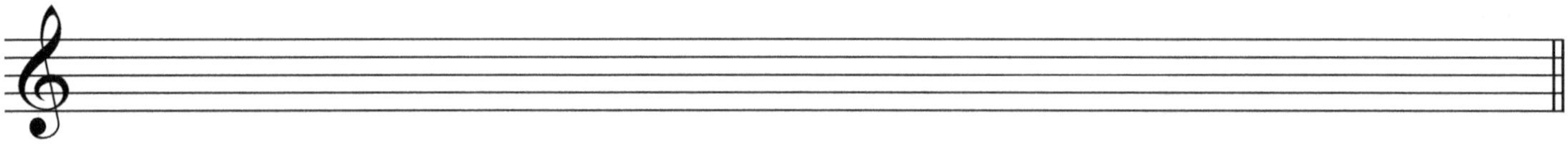

A major

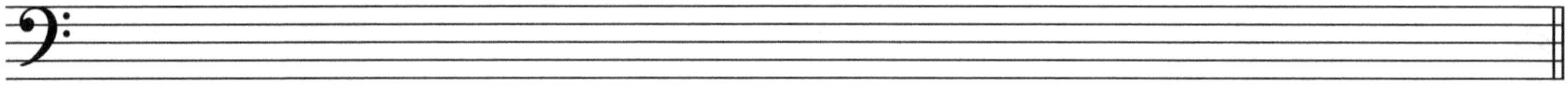

A♭ major

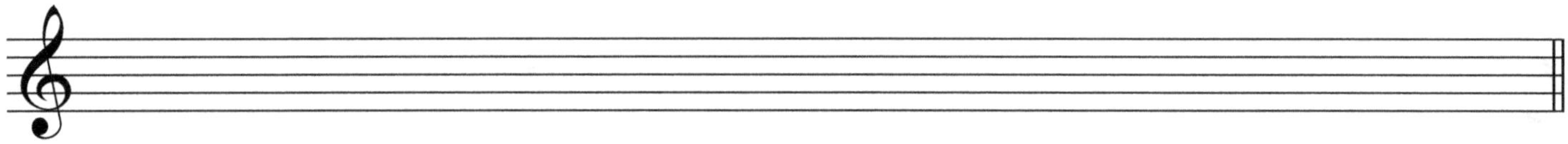

C♯ major

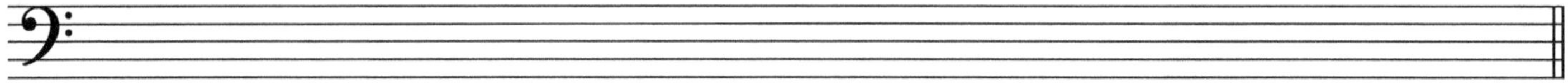

G♭ major

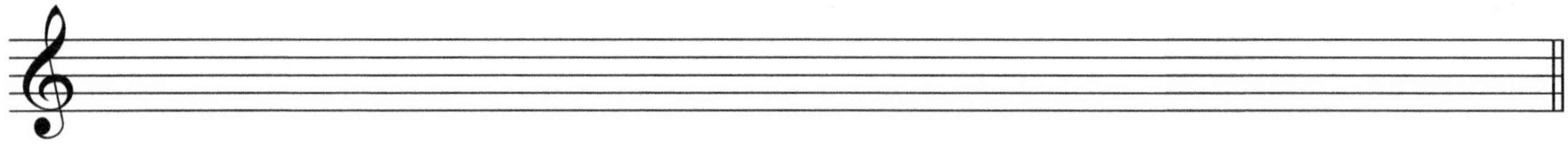

D♭ major

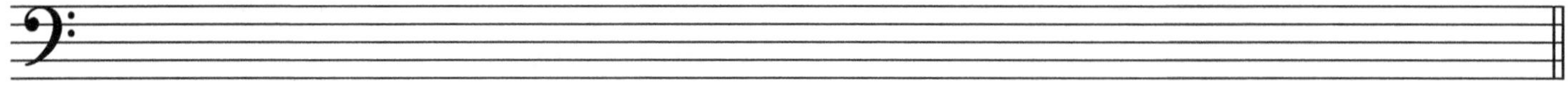

3. Write the following scales in whole notes, ascending and descending, using key signatures.

The scale with C♯ as the dominant

The major scale with the key signature of six flats

The major scale with B♭ as the leading tone

The major scale with the key signature of two sharps

The major scale with F as the supertonic

The major scale with a key signature of three sharps

The major scale with F as the mediant

The major scale with D♭ as the subdominant

4. For the following key signatures, name the major key and identify the degree of the scale for the given note.

key: _____   _____   _____   _____

degree: _____   _____   _____   _____

key: _____   _____   _____   _____

degree: _____   _____   _____   _____

key: _____   _____   _____   _____

degree: _____   _____   _____   _____

key: _____   _____   _____   _____

degree: _____   _____   _____   _____

key: _____   _____   _____   _____

degree: _____   _____   _____   _____

Minor Scales

For each major key, there is a **relative minor key**. Major and minor keys that are related use the same key signature. The relative minor of a major key is three half steps *lower*.

Relative Major and Minor Keys

Major Keys	Sharps and Flats	Minor Keys
C	-	A
G	F♯	E
D	F♯, C♯	B
A	F♯, C♯, G♯	F♯
E	F♯, C♯, G♯, D♯	C♯
B	F♯, C♯, G♯, D♯, A♯	G♯
F♯	F♯, C♯, G♯, D♯, A♯, E♯	D♯
C♯	F♯, C♯, G♯, D♯, A♯, E♯, B♯	A♯
F	B♭	D
B♭	B♭, E♭	G
E♭	B♭, E♭, A♭	C
A♭	B♭, E♭, A♭, D♭	F
D♭	B♭, E♭, A♭, D♭, G♭	B♭
G♭	B♭, E♭, A♭, D♭, G♭, C♭	E♭
C♭	B♭, E♭, A♭, D♭, G♭, C♭, F♭	A♭

A major scale and a minor scale that have the same tonic are called **tonic major** and **tonic minor**. For example, F major is the tonic major of F minor and F minor is the tonic minor of F major.

When a minor scale is written with no accidentals, it is called a **natural minor scale**.

D natural minor scale

The **harmonic minor scale** is formed by raising the seventh degree ($\hat{7}$) of the natural minor scale.

D harmonic minor scale

The **melodic minor scale** is formed by raising the sixth ($\hat{6}$) and seventh ($\hat{7}$) degrees of the natural minor scale ascending, and lowering the sixth ($\hat{6}$) and seventh ($\hat{7}$) degrees descending.

D melodic minor scale

1. Name the key and type (natural, harmonic, melodic) of the following minor scales.

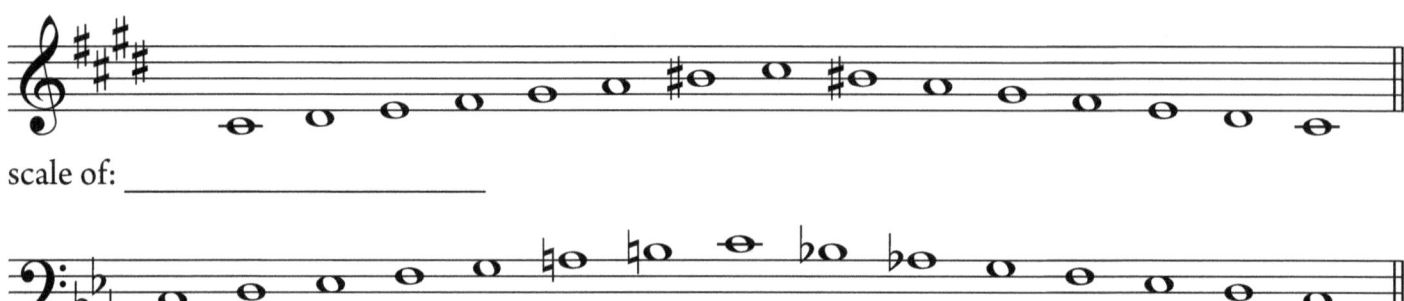
scale of: _____

scale of: _____

scale of: _____

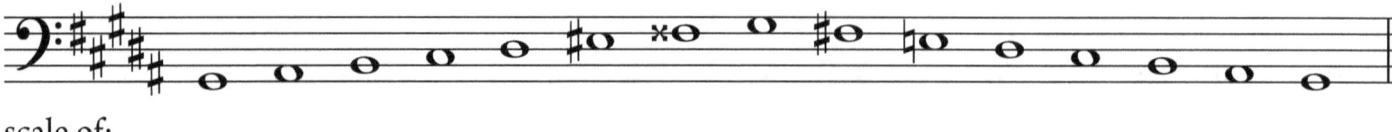
scale of: _____

scale of: _____

2. Write the following scales, ascending and descending, using key signatures.

D harmonic minor in half notes

C# melodic minor in eighth notes

F natural minor in quarter notes

E melodic minor in whole notes

F# harmonic minor in sixteenth notes

C melodic minor in dotted half notes

G# harmonic minor in sixteenth notes

E♭ natural minor in whole notes.

3. Name the minor keys for the following key signatures.

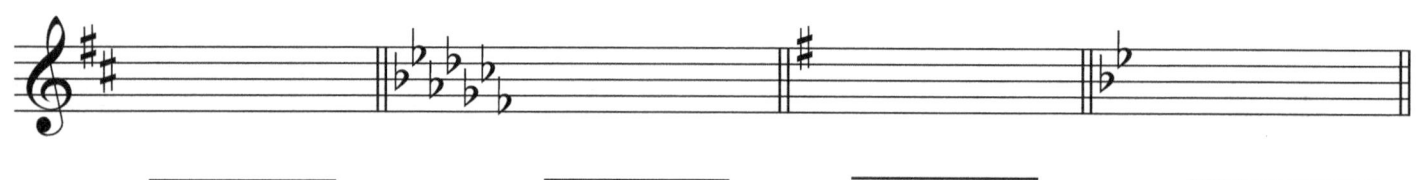

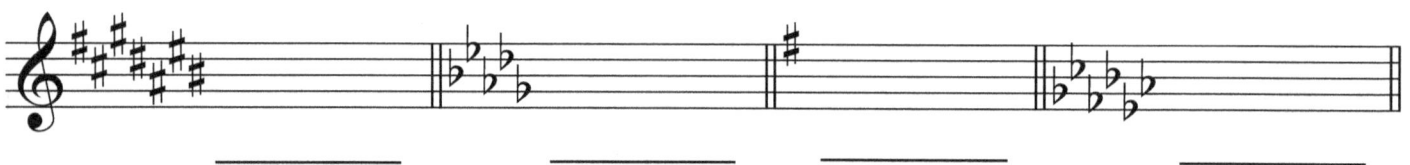

4. Name the relative minors of the following major keys.

F# major	_____	B♭ major	_____
G major	_____	E♭ major	_____
C# major	_____	E major	_____
A♭ major	_____	D♭ major	_____
C major	_____	F major	_____
B major	_____	G♭ major	_____
A major	_____	C♭ major	_____
D major	_____		

5. Write the following scales, ascending and descending, using the correct key signature.

A major

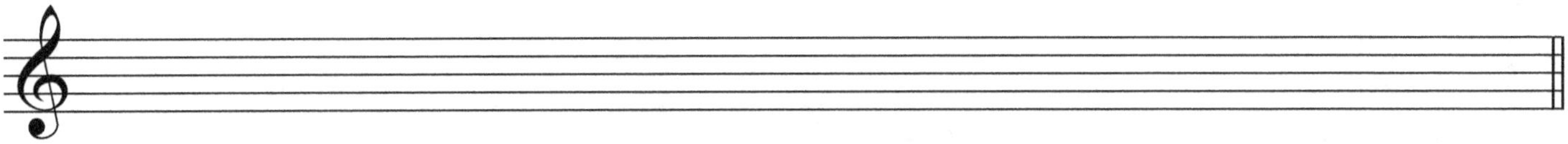

The relative melodic minor of A major

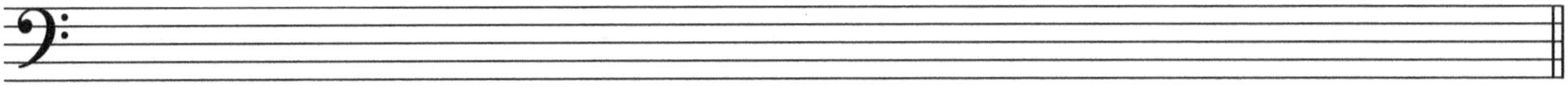

The tonic harmonic minor of A major

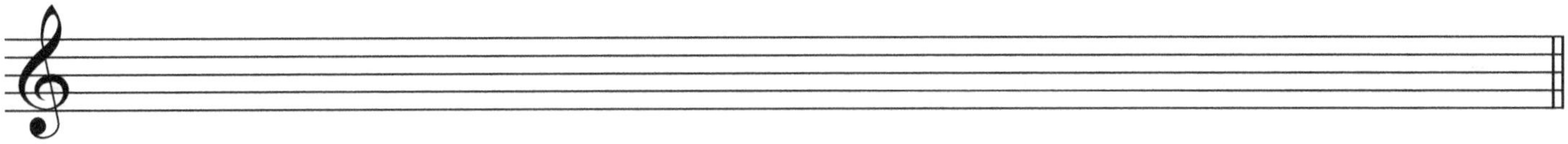

F♯ major from dominant to dominant

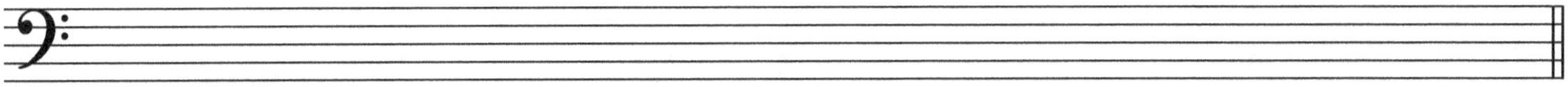

E♭ major from supertonic to supertonic

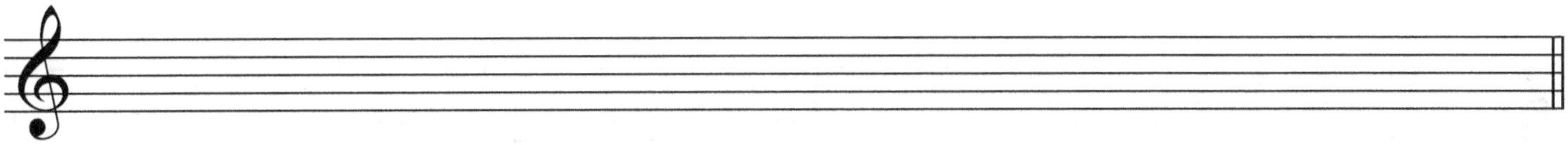

G harmonic minor from leading tone to leading tone

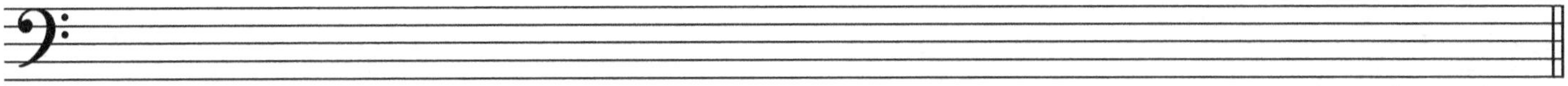

B♭ melodic minor

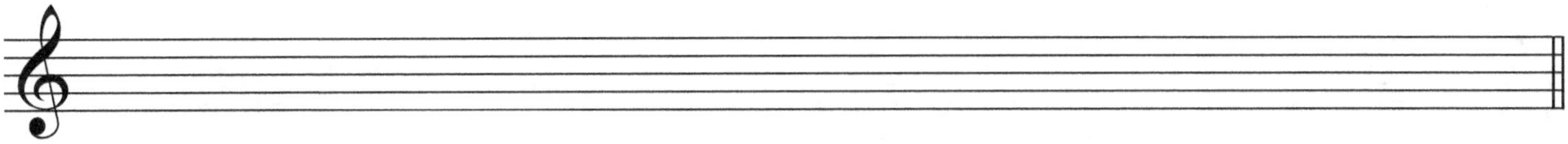

The tonic major of B♭ minor

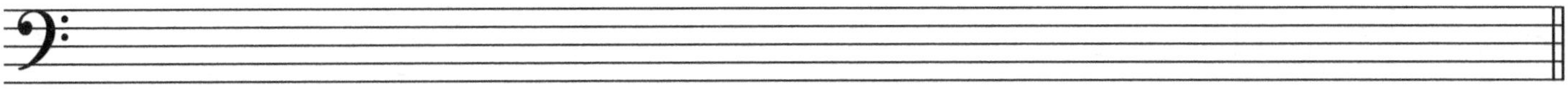

6. Write the following scales, ascending and descending, using accidentals instead of a key signature.

The relative minor, harmonic form, of D♭ major

The tonic minor, melodic form, of C major

F♯ natural minor from submediant to submediant

B harmonic minor from tonic to tonic

The melodic minor with G♯ as the dominant

The natural minor with E as the supertonic

G♭ major from mediant to mediant

C♯ major

7. Add clefs, key signatures and any necessary accidentals to form the following scales.

F harmonic minor

Db major

Eb melodic minor

C# natural minor

B major

G# harmonic minor

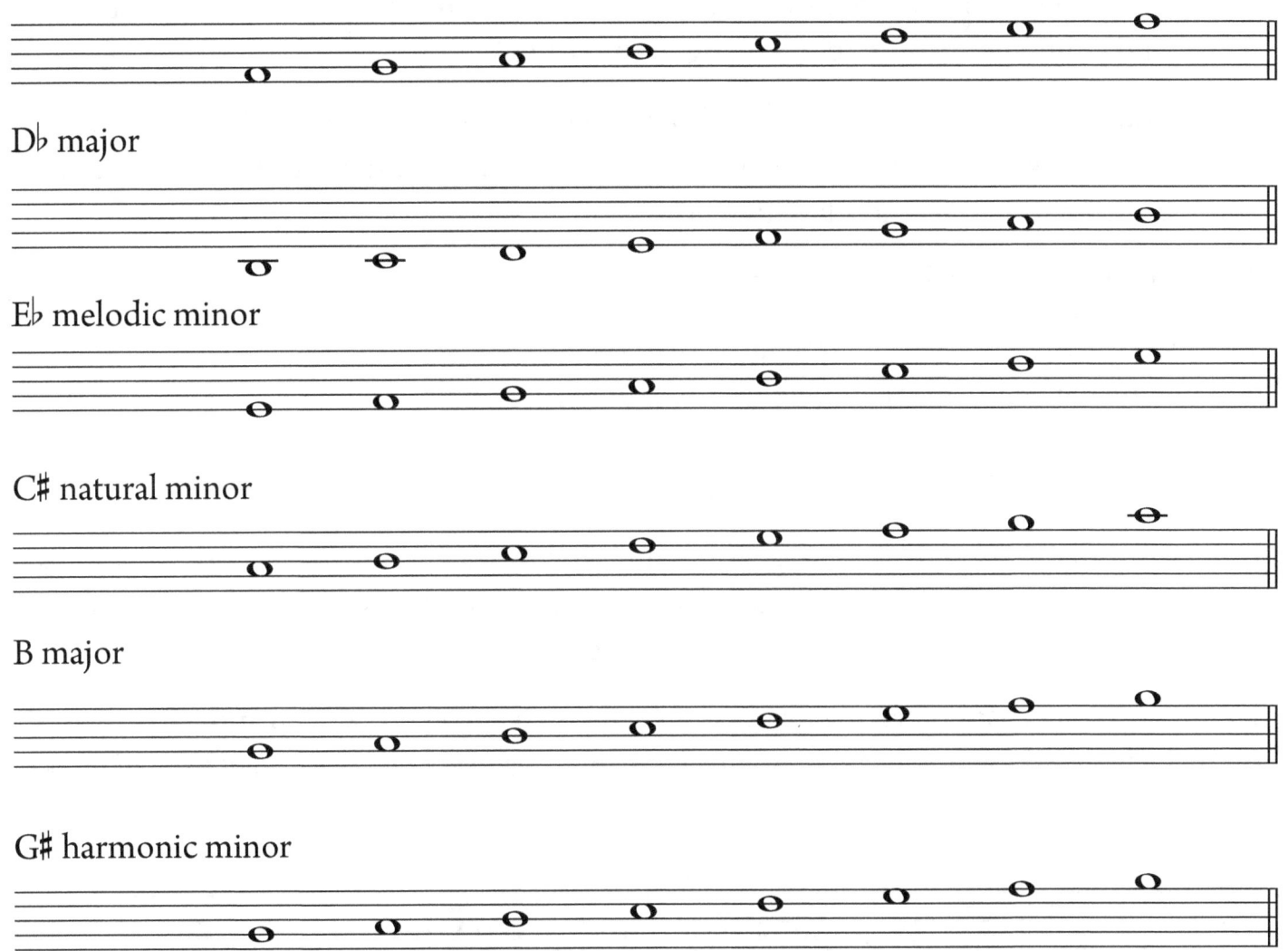

8. Learn the following Italian terms and definitions.

animato	lively, animated
brillante	brilliant
con	with
con brio	with vigour, spirit
con espressione	with expression
espressivo	expressive, with expression
leggiero	light, nimble, quick
spiritoso	spirited
tranquillo	quiet, tranquil

Chromatic Scales

Major and minor scales are **diatonic**. They are made up of whole steps and half steps and contain only notes that belong to the scale.

A **chromatic scale** is made up of only half steps and contains all twelve notes in the octave. There are two types of chromatic scales: The chromatic scale that has no key signature, and the chromatic scale that is based on a key.

There are two simple rules for chromatic scales.

1. Never use the same letter name more than twice.
2. Do not change the name of the tonic note enharmonically.

Chromatic Scales Without a Key Signature

In this chromatic scale without a key signature, the notes are *raised going up* and *lowered going down*. When you write this type of scale, you use sharps as soon as possible on the way up, and flats as soon as possible on the way down.

Here's a chromatic scale starting on see C. Sharps are used on the way up and flats are used on the way down. *Notice that the bar line in the middle cancels all the accidentals used on the way up.*

In the following scale (F sharp chromatic), all the descending accidentals are flats except the last note. Since F sharp is the starting note, F sharp must also be the final note. You cannot change the name of the starting note enharmonically (i.e. to G flat).

Here's a chromatic scale starting on D flat. This scale must begin with flats but it changes to sharps as soon as possible on the way up. Flats are used all the way down.

1. Write the following scales, ascending and descending, using accidentals instead of a key signature.

Chromatic scale starting on E

Chromatic scale starting on A♭

Chromatic scale starting on C♯

Chromatic scale starting on B♭

Chromatic scale starting on G

Chromatic scale starting on E♭

Chromatic scale starting on D

Chromatic scale starting on G♯

Chromatic Scales Based on a Key

A chromatic scale may also be based on a major scale. This form of chromatic scale may be written with or without a key signature.

To write this type of chromatic scale without a key signature, follow these three steps:

1. Determine the tonic and dominant notes by using the first note as the tonic of the major scale. Write the tonic and dominant notes, ascending and descending.

In the example below, the scale begins on E. The tonic and dominant notes of E major are E and B.

2. Write each of the remaining notes *twice*.

3. Add the necessary accidentals to form a chromatic scale.

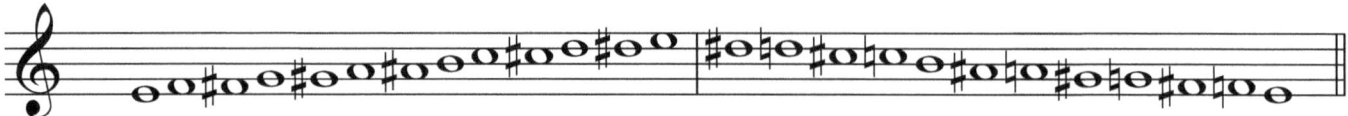

To write this type of chromatic scale with the key signature, use the key signature of the major key of the starting note. In the example below, the starting note is E, so use the key signature of E major. *Notice the difference in the pattern of accidentals between this scale and the one that has no key signature*

2. Write the following scale, ascending and descending using a key signature.

Chromatic scale starting on F

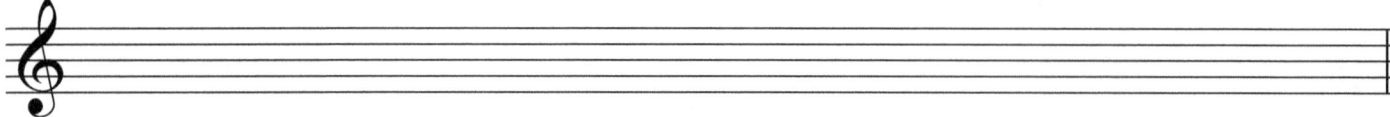

3. Write the following chromatic scales, ascending and descending.

Chromatic scale starting on G

Chromatic scale starting on A♭, using a key signature

Chromatic scale starting on B

Chromatic scale starting on D, using a key signature

Chromatic scale starting on D♭

Chromatic scale starting on G, using a key signature

Chromatic scale starting on F

Chromatic scale starting on C♯ using a key signature

Whole Tone Scales

The whole tone scale is made up of whole steps. A whole tone scale can begin on any note, but all whole tone scales are based on one or the other of two forms.

One starts on C.

The other form starts on C sharp or D flat.

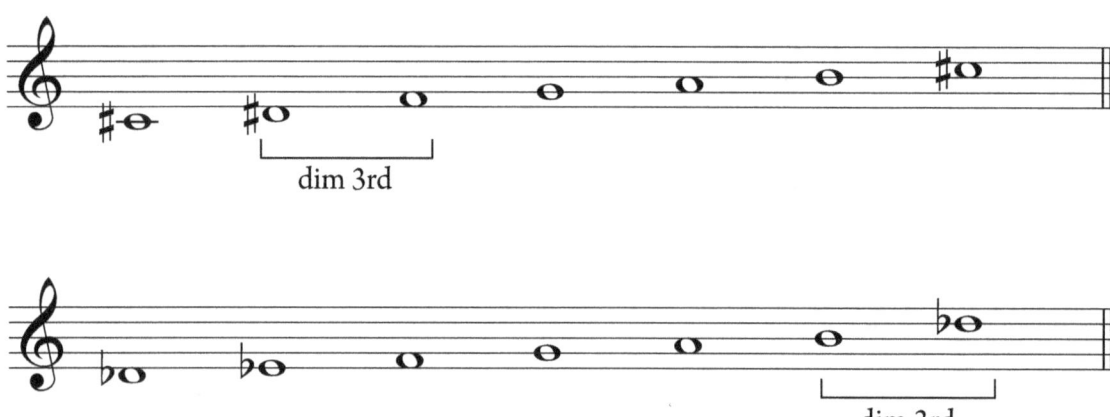

A few important points to remember when writing whole tone scales:

- Whole tone scales use six different letter names.
- Do not enharmonically change the name of the starting note.
- Do not mix sharps and flats in the same scale: use all sharps or all flats.
- Every whole tone scale contains the interval of the diminished third. (See the chapter on intervals).

Since the notes of a whole tone scale are spaced evenly, any note can function as the tonic. Music based on a whole tone scale has a feeling of restlessness because of the ambiguity of the tonic. A number of 20th century composers including Claude Debussy, used whole tone scales in their music.

1. Add accidentals to the following to create whole tone scales.

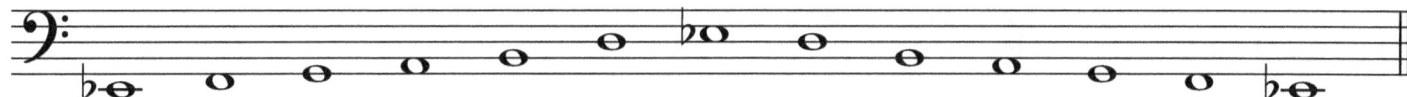

2. Write the following whole tone scales, ascending and descending.

The whole tone scale starting on F

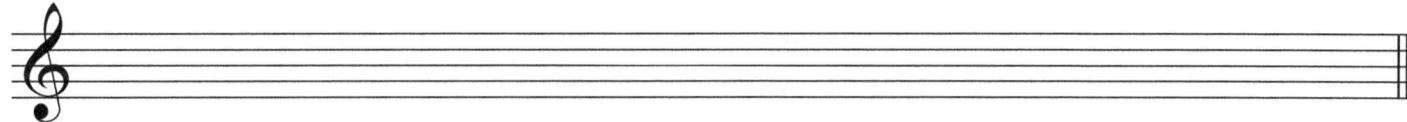

The whole tone scale starting on D♯

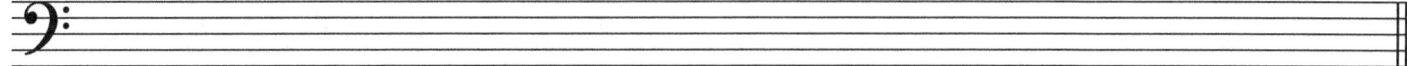

The whole tone scale starting on E♭

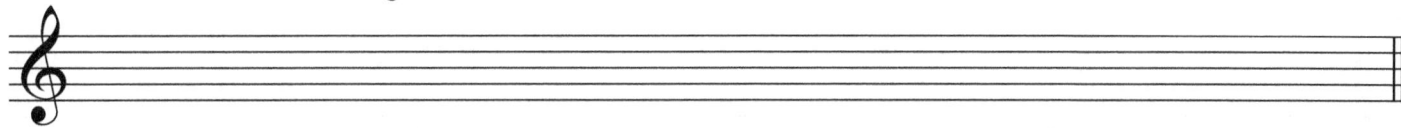

The whole tone scale starting on A

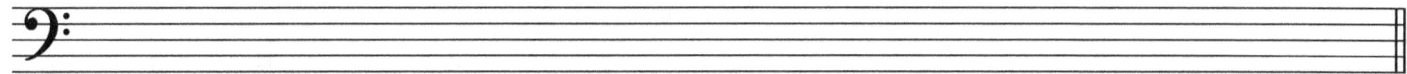

The whole tone scale starting on E

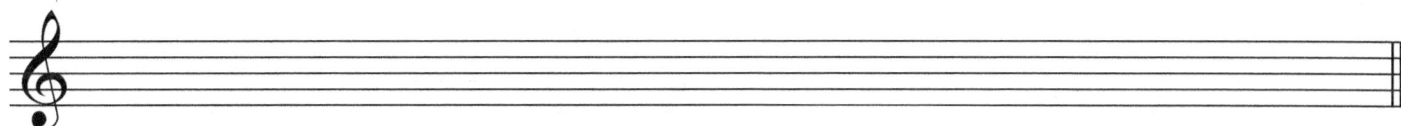

The whole tone scale starting on F♯

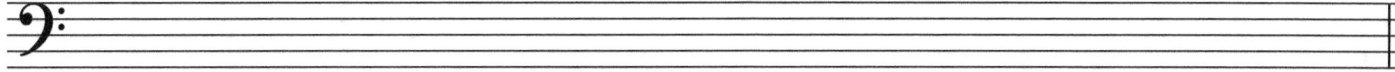

The Blues Scale

> Blues is an African-American music genre characterized by a scale in which certain notes are lowered. A blues tune is usually 12 measures long and consists of three four measure phrases.
>
> Here is a basic blues scale.
>
>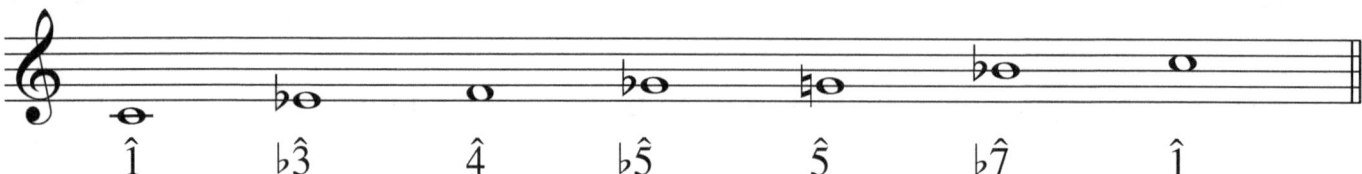
>
> If you compare this scale to a major scale, you will find three differences:
>
> 1. The second and sixth degree are missing.
> 2. The third, fifth, and seventh degrees are lowered by a half step. These are called "blue" notes.
> 3. The fifth degree of the scale occurs twice (once lowered and once unaltered).

1. Write the following blues scales, ascending only.

B♭ blues

C blues

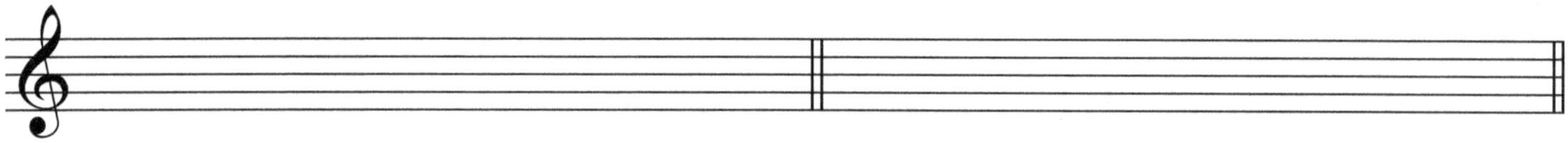

F blues

A blues

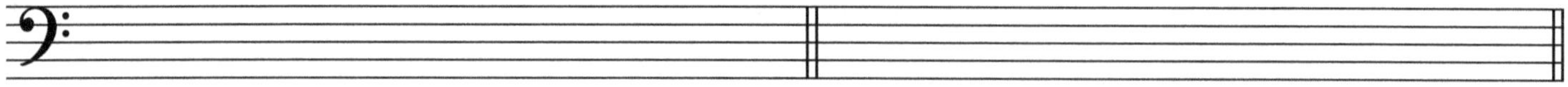

G blues

B blues

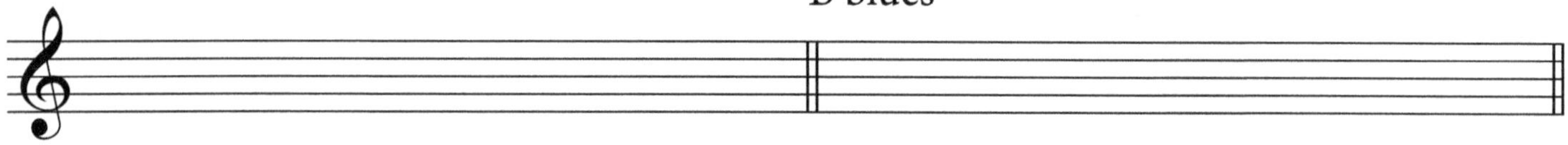

D blues

E blues

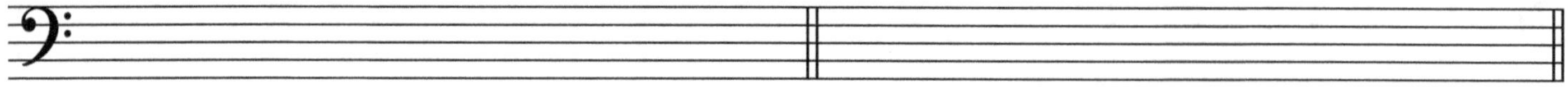

31

The following piece is an example of the blues in C. The melody of *Cool Blue* is made up of notes from the C blues scale. Practice the C blues scale and then play this piece.

Using the same left-hand bass part and the C blues scale, improvise your own blues. Use different rhythms and make up your own patterns.

Cool Blue

Mark Sarnecki

Pentatonic Scales

The **pentatonic scale** consists of five notes, and is one of the oldest scales in existence. It was found in Asian music as early as 2000 B.C., and is common in folk music. Pentatonic scales were also used by some composers in the 19th and 20th centuries. A **major pentatonic scale** can be formed by removing the fourth and seventh degrees of a major scale.

C major pentatonic

F♯ major pentatonic

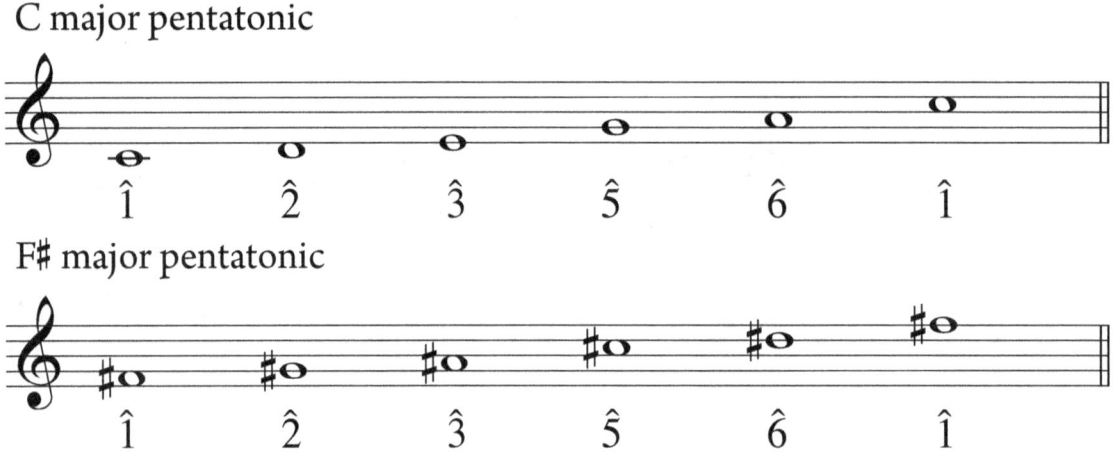

1. Write the following major pentatonic scales, ascending only.

D major pentatonic — A♭ major pentatonic

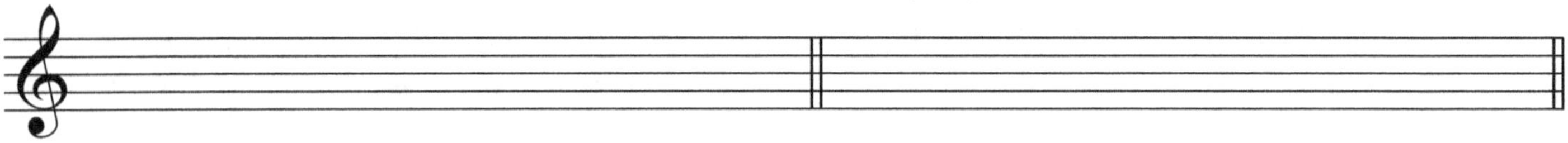

F major pentatonic — E major pentatonic

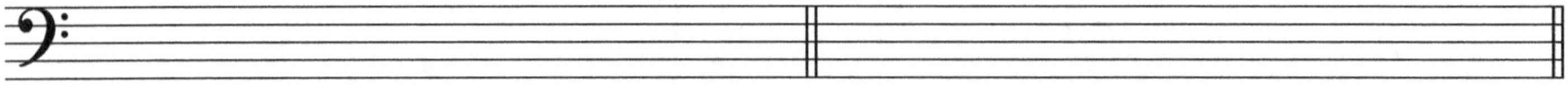

B♭ major pentatonic — C♯ major pentatonic

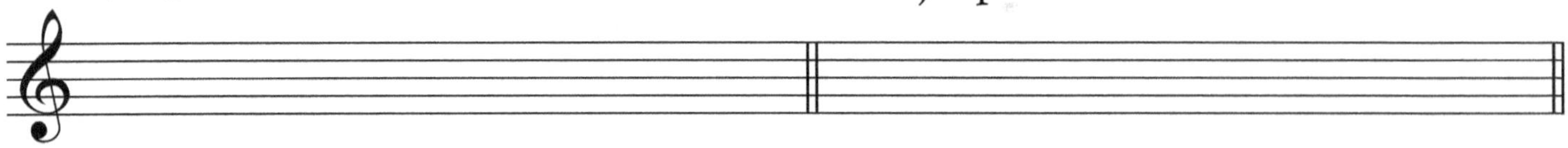

B major pentatonic — G major pentatonic

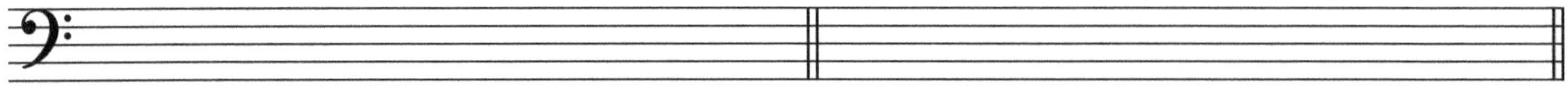

The **minor pentatonic scale** can be formed by removing the second and sixth degrees from a natural minor scale. The minor pentatonic scale always begins with the interval of a minor 3rd.

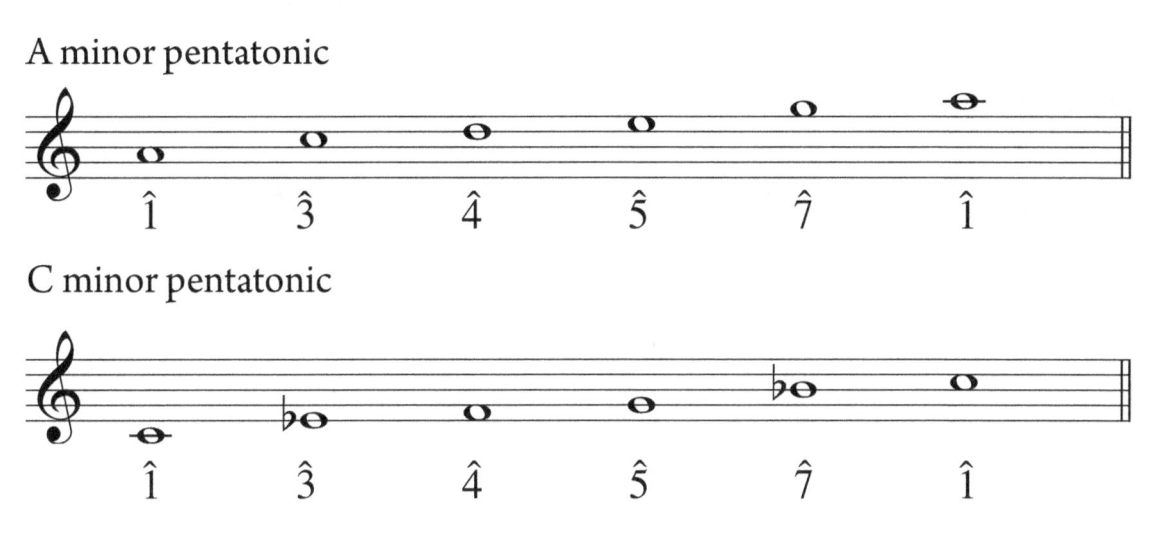

The following folk melody is based on the E minor pentatonic scale. Write the E minor pentatonic scale in the staff below, ascending and descending. Play Land of the Silver Birch and listen carefully for the pentatonic melody.

Land of the Silver Birch

Folk Melody

2. Write the following minor pentatonic scales, ascending and descending.

G minor pentatonic

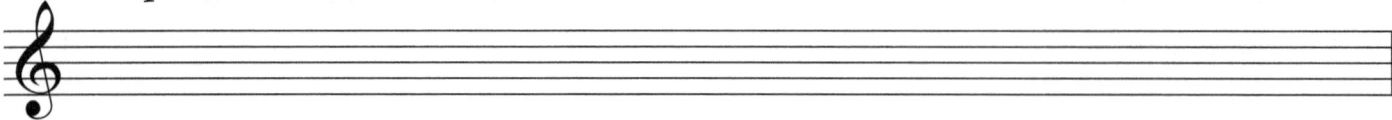

D minor pentatonic

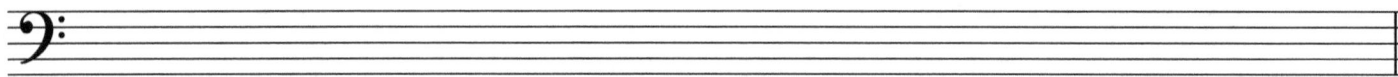

F minor pentatonic

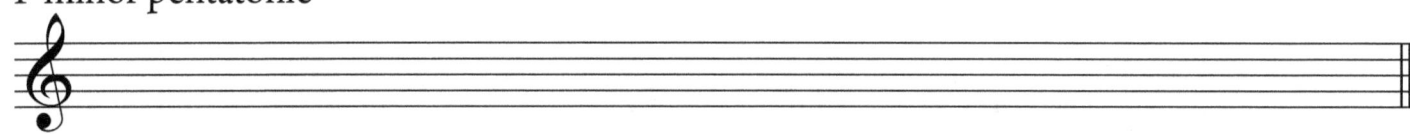

B minor pentatonic

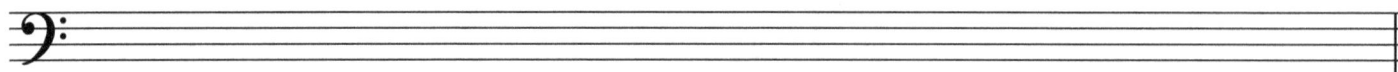

The Octatonic Scale

The octatonic scale is an eight note scale in which whole steps and half steps alternate. This scale is used prominently in the music of several composers, including Nikolai Rimsky-Korsakov, Igor Stravinsky, and Béla Bartók. It begins and ends on the same note, so like all scales, the tonic must not be changed enharmonically. This scale can begin with either a whole step or a half step. Only three transpositions of the octatonic scale are possible. An octatonic scale starting on any note will have the same pitches as one of the three octatonic scales shown below.

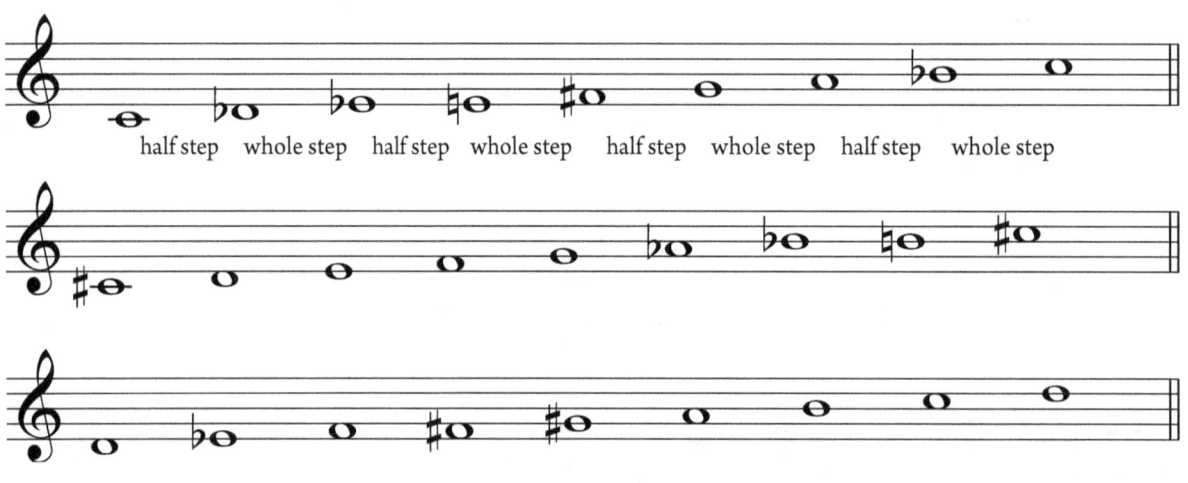

1. Write the following octatonic scales, ascending and descending.

On F, starting with a whole step

On B, starting with a half step

On D, starting with a whole step

On E, starting with a half step

On A, starting with a half step

IDENTIFYING SCALES

1. Name each of the following scales as major, natural minor, harmonic minor, melodic minor, whole tone, major pentatonic, minor pentatonic, chromatic, blues, or octatonic.

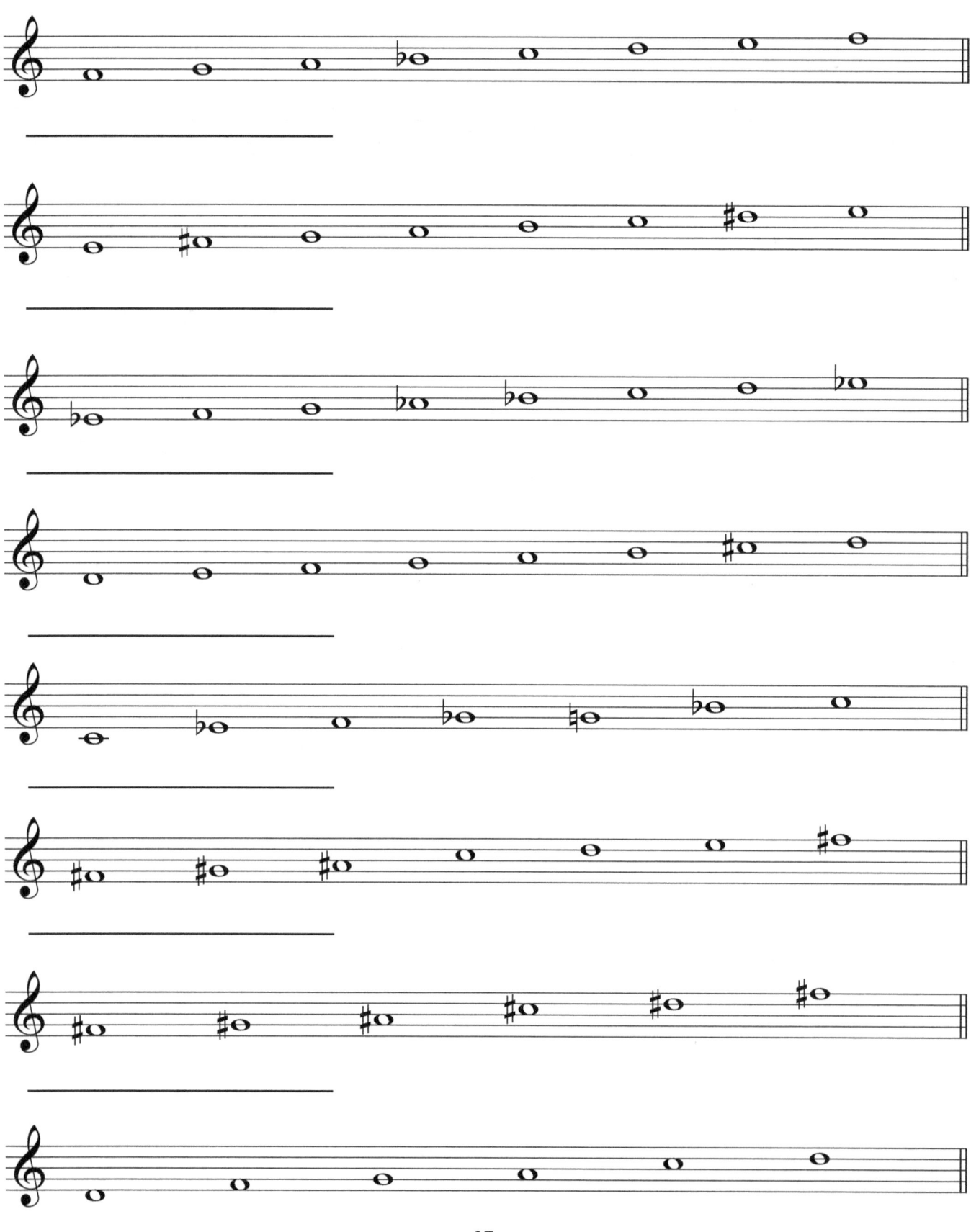

2. Name each of the following scales as major, natural minor, harmonic minor, melodic minor, whole tone, major pentatonic, minor pentatonic, chromatic, blues, or octatonic.

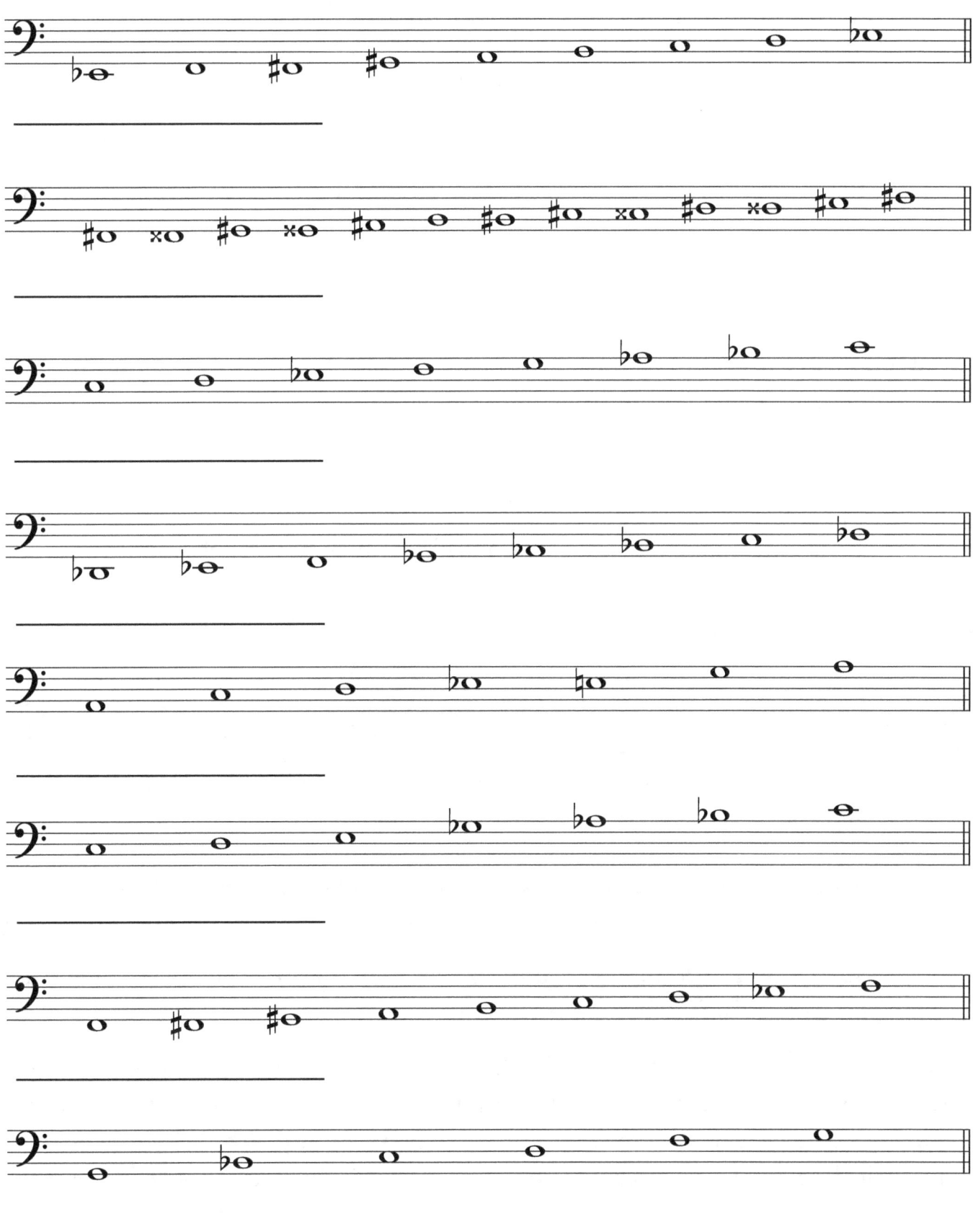

INTERVALS

An interval is the distance between two notes. When the notes of an interval are played one after the other, the interval is called **melodic**.

When the notes of an interval are played at the same time, the interval is called **harmonic**.

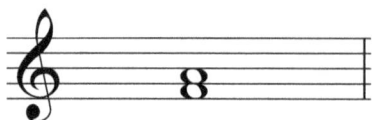

All intervals have a specific number. This number is determined by counting the letter names of the notes in the interval from the lowest to the highest.

There are *five* letter names from C to G.
(C - D - E - F - G)
Therefore, C to G is an interval of a fifth.

The following intervals are formed between the notes of the major scale.

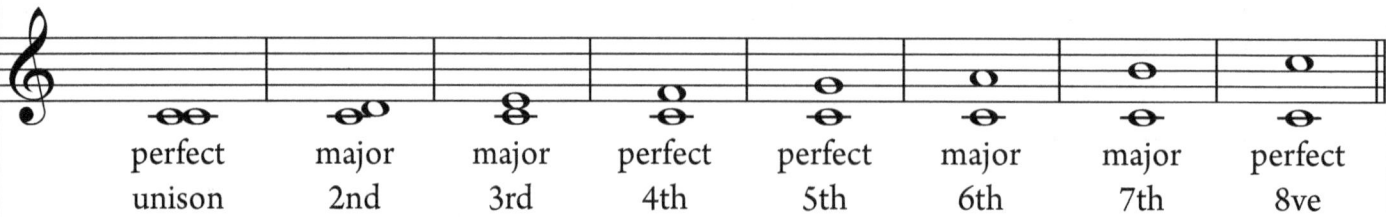

The intervals of a unison, 4th, 5th, and octave are classified as **perfect intervals**. The abbreviation for a perfect interval is "per"... for example, per 4.

The intervals of a 2nd, 3rd, 6th, and 7th are classified as **major intervals**. The abbreviation for a major interval is "maj"... for example, maj 3.

Think of the bottom note of an interval as the tonic of a major scale. If the upper note of the interval is a member of the scale of the lower note, the interval will be either perfect or major. For example, D to F sharp is a major 3rd because F sharp is the third note of the D major scale. F to B flat is a perfect fourth because B-flat is the fourth note of the F major scale.

A **minor interval** is one half step smaller than a major interval. In other words, the notes of a minor interval are *one half step closer together* than the notes of a major interval. The abbreviation for a minor interval is "min"... for example min 3rd.

Note that only 2nds, 3rds, 6ths, and 7ths can be minor intervals.

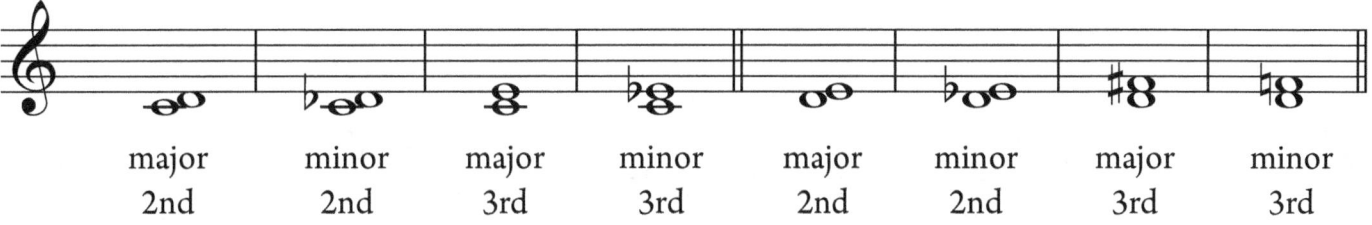

To determine if an interval is major or minor, think of the bottom note as the tonic of a major scale. If the top note is a member of the major scale of the bottom note, the interval is major. If the top note is a half step lower, the interval is minor.

For example, D to F natural is a 3rd, but F natural is not part of the scale of D major. The interval of D to F natural is one half step smaller than the major 3rd of D to F sharp. This makes D to F a minor third.

A major interval can be made minor by lowering the top note or raising the bottom note by *one half step*.

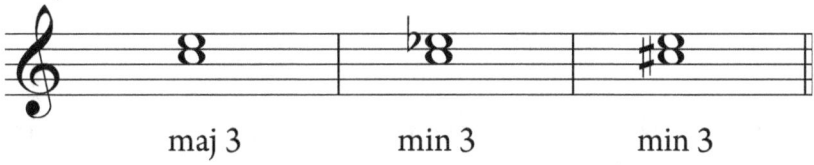

An **augmented interval** is one half step larger than a perfect or major interval. In other words, the notes of an augmented interval are one half step further apart than the notes of a perfect or major interval. The abbreviation for an augmented interval is "aug".... for example, aug 4.

A perfect or major interval can be made augmented by raising the top note or lowering the bottom note by one half step.

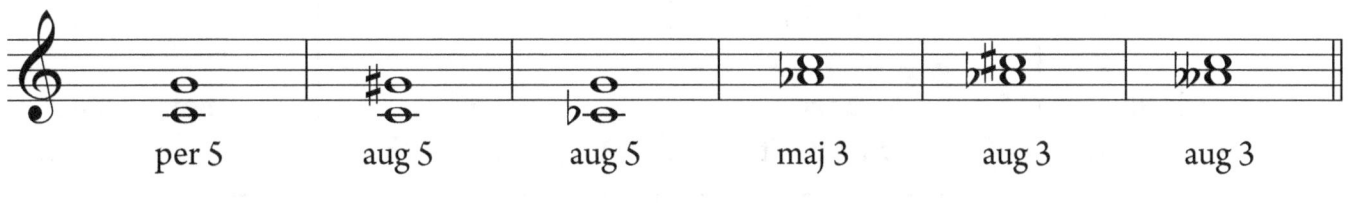

A **diminished interval** is one half step smaller than either a *perfect interval* or a *minor interval*. In other words, the notes of a diminished interval are one half step closer together than the notes of a perfect or minor interval. The abbreviation for a diminished interval is "dim"... for example, dim 5.

A perfect interval can be made diminished by lowering the top note or raising the bottom note by *one half step*.

A minor interval can be made diminished by lowering the top note or raising the bottom note by *one half step*.

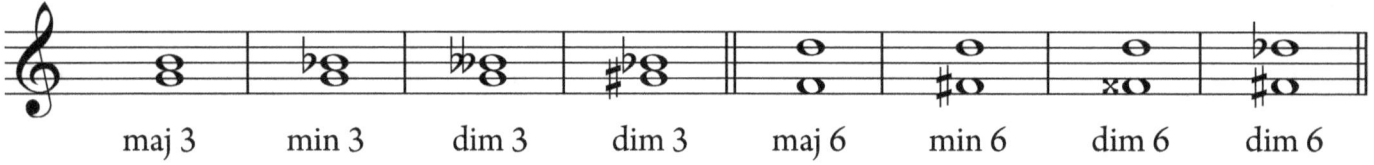

Note that a diminished interval is *one half step smaller than a perfect interval, but two half steps smaller than a major interval.*

Here is a summary of the relationship between the various types of intervals. The starting point is the note in the major scale.

MINUS two half steps	MINUS one half step	Note in the MAJOR SCALE	PLUS one half step
	Diminished unison, 4th, 5th, 8ve	**Perfect** unison, 4th, 5th, 8ve	**Augmented** unison, 4th, 5th, 8ve
Diminished 2nd, 3rd, 6th, 7th	**Minor** 2nd, 3rd, 6th, 7th	**Major** 2nd, 3rd, 6th, 7th	**Augmented** 2nd, 3rd, 6th, 7th

1. Name the following intervals, then rewrite each as an augmented interval by changing the upper note.

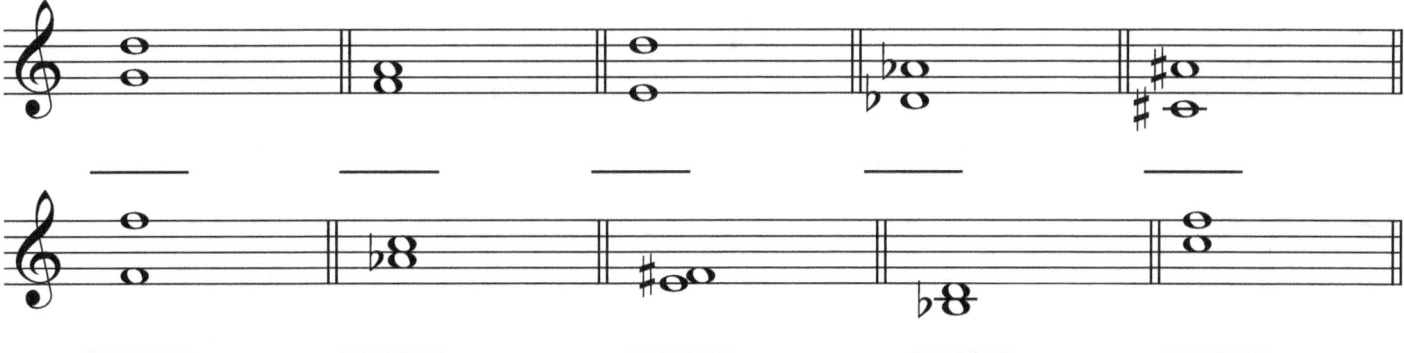

2. Name the following intervals, then rewrite each as an augmented interval by changing the lower note.

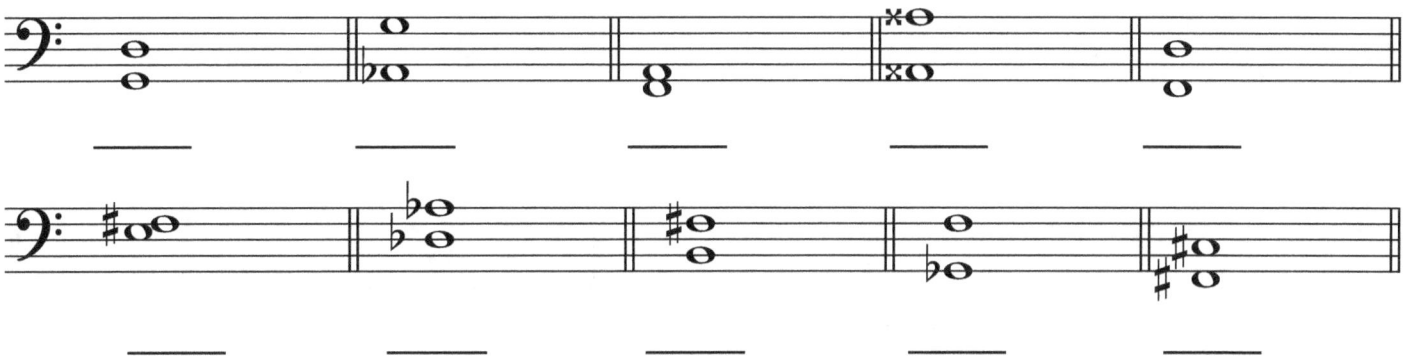

3. Name the following intervals, then rewrite each as a diminished interval by changing the upper note.

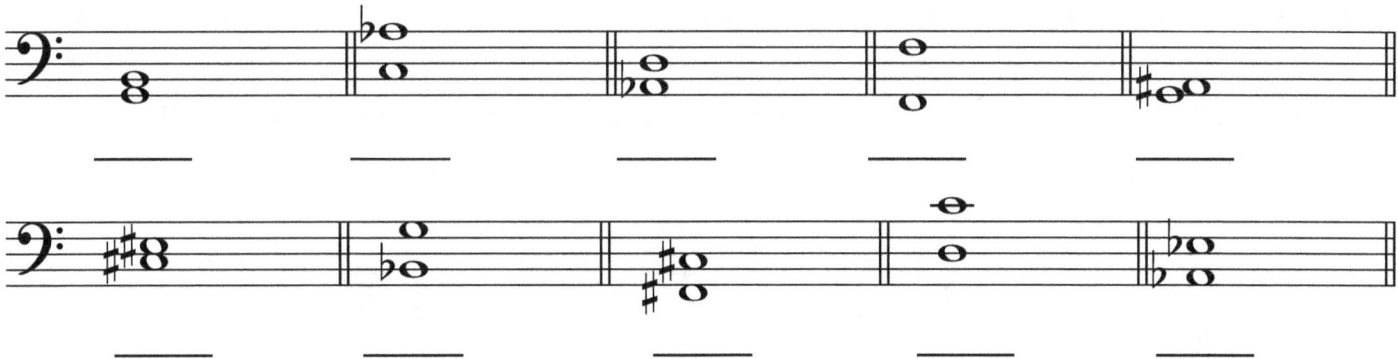

4. Name the following intervals, then rewrite each as a diminished interval by changing the lower note.

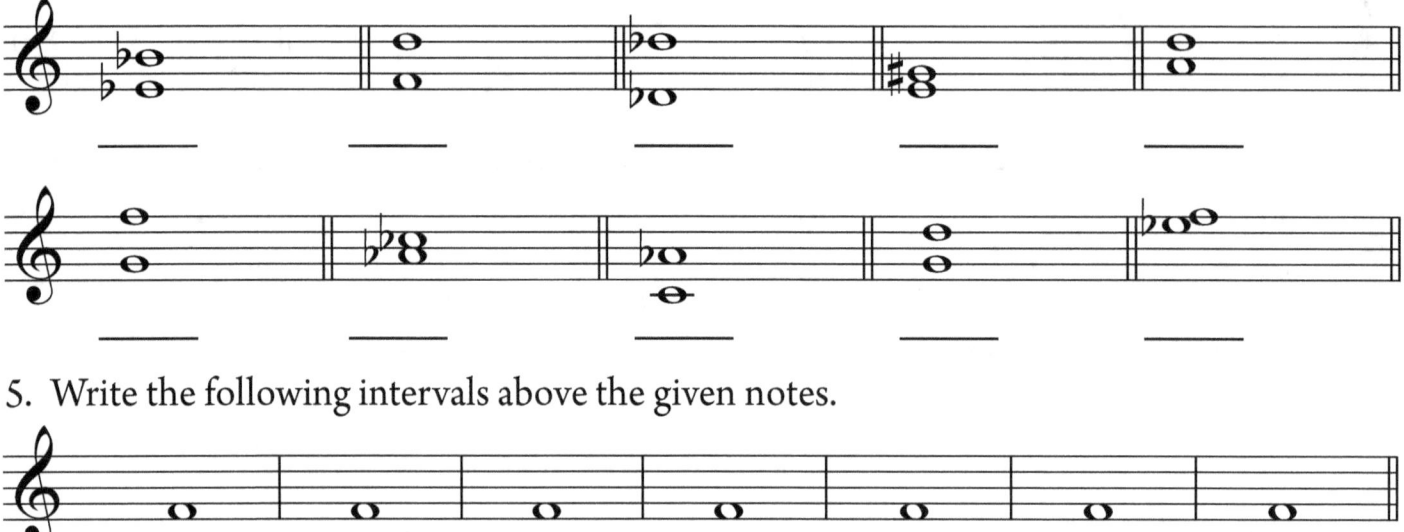

5. Write the following intervals above the given notes.

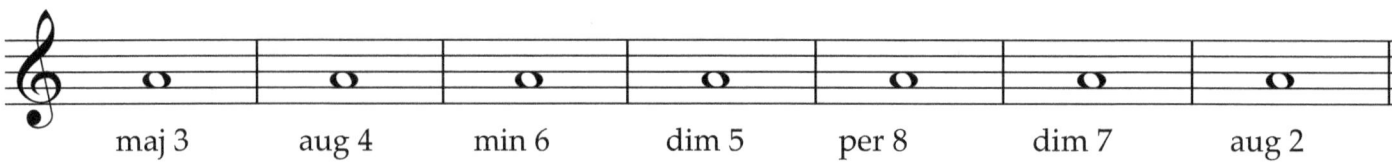

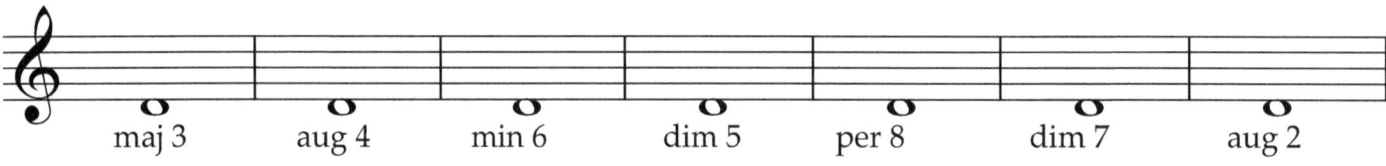

We consider the perfect unison the smallest interval, even though a unison is not really an interval. An interval is defined as the distance between two notes. There is no distance between the notes of a unison. The unison requires special consideration. Since there is no distance between the notes of a unison, it cannot be made smaller. Unisons can never be diminished intervals. If any note of a unison is altered, the notes become further away from each other, and it becomes augmented.

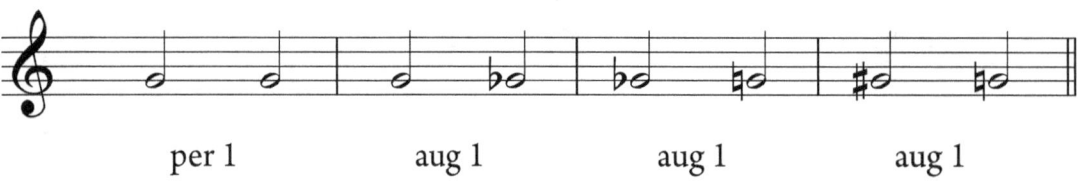

Sometimes the lowest note of an interval is not the tonic of a major key. For instance, in the examples below, we know that D sharp to A sharp is a fifth, but there is no such key as D sharp major.

In order to name the interval, we must follow three steps:

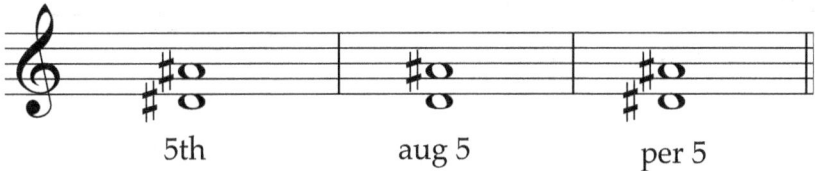

1. Lower the bottom note to the note that is the tonic of an existing key. *Note that this note has the same letter name, so the number of the interval remains the same.* In the example above, we lowered D sharp one half step to D.

2. Name the new interval. The interval of D to A sharp is an augmented 5th.

3. Move the lower note back up to its original pitch. By raising the lower note, we have made the interval one half step smaller. A perfect 5th is one half step smaller than an augmented 5th, so the interval of D sharp to A sharp must be a perfect 5th.

1. Name the following intervals.

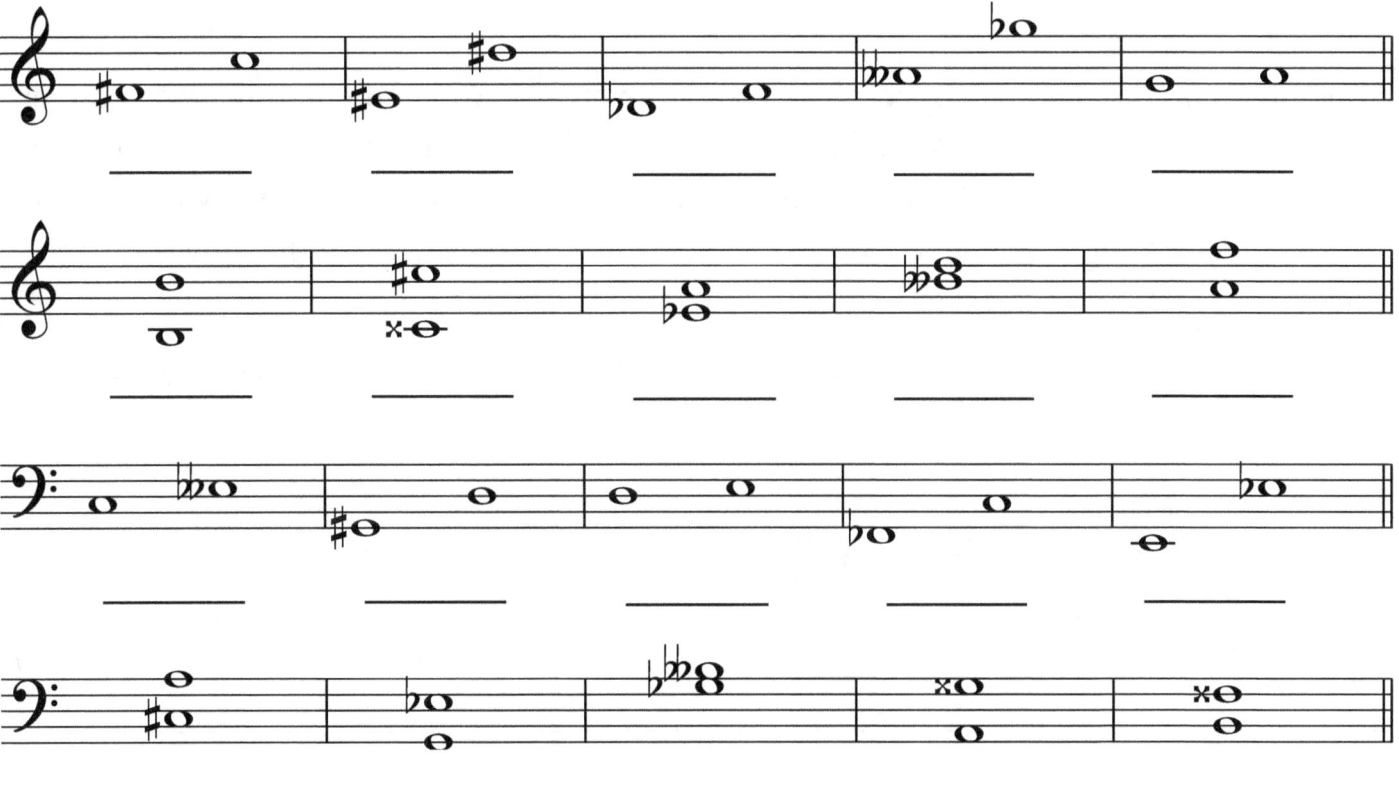

Inversion

When an interval is turned upside down, it is **inverted**. For example, when the interval of G to B is inverted, it becomes B to G.

There are two ways to invert an interval:

1. Write the lower note above the upper note.
2. Write the upper note below the lower note.

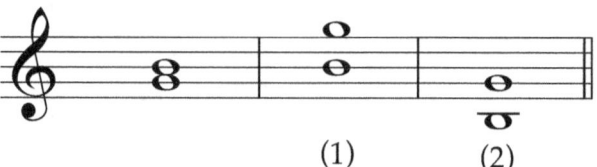

When an interval is inverted:

major	becomes	**minor**
minor	becomes	**major**
augmented	becomes	**diminished**
diminished	becomes	**augmented**
perfect	remains	**perfect**

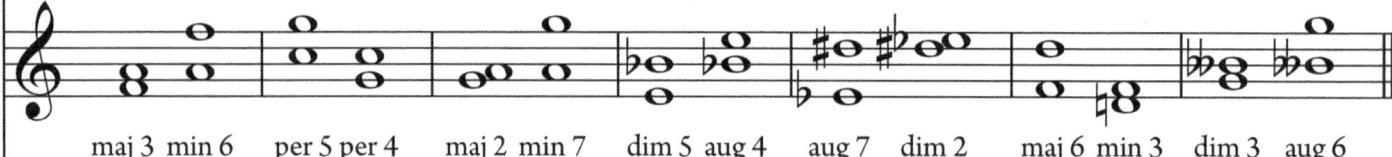

maj 3 min 6   per 5 per 4   maj 2 min 7   dim 5 aug 4   aug 7 dim 2   maj 6 min 3   dim 3 aug 6

Note that the number of an interval *plus* the number of its inversion always equals nine.

The augmented octave is a special case when inverting. An augmented octave is larger than an octave and when it is inverted the numbers do not add up to 9. The example below shows the inversion of the augmented octave. An aug 8 becomes a dim 8 when inverted. An inverted aug 8 *cannot* become a dim 1 because, as we learned in the previous pages, there is no such thing as a dim 1.

However, since a dim 8 is smaller than an octave, it becomes an aug 1 when inverted.

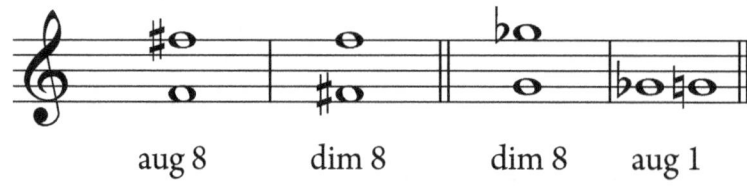

aug 8   dim 8   dim 8   aug 1

2. Name the following intervals. Invert them and name the inversions.

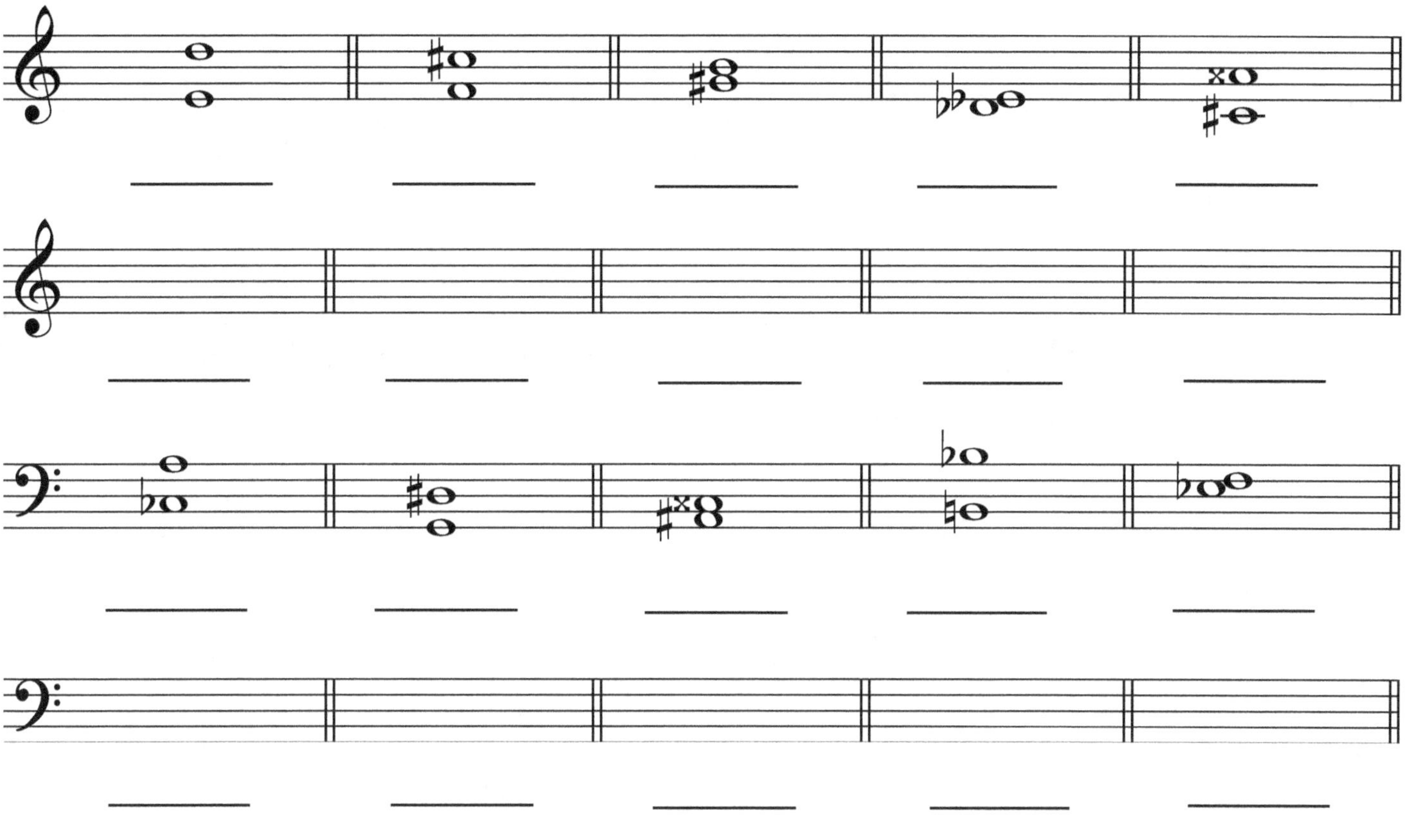

3. Write the following intervals above the given notes. Invert each interval and name the inversion.

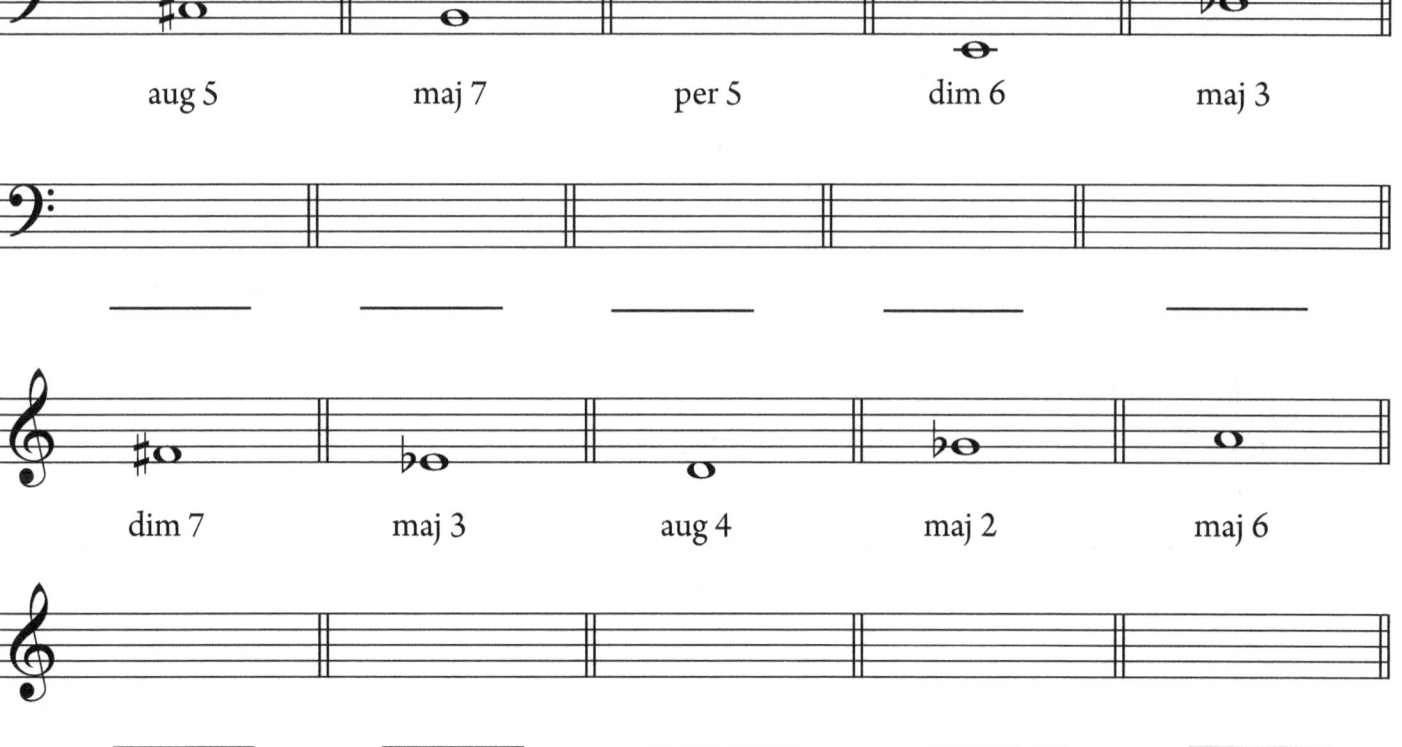

4. Write the following intervals above the given notes.

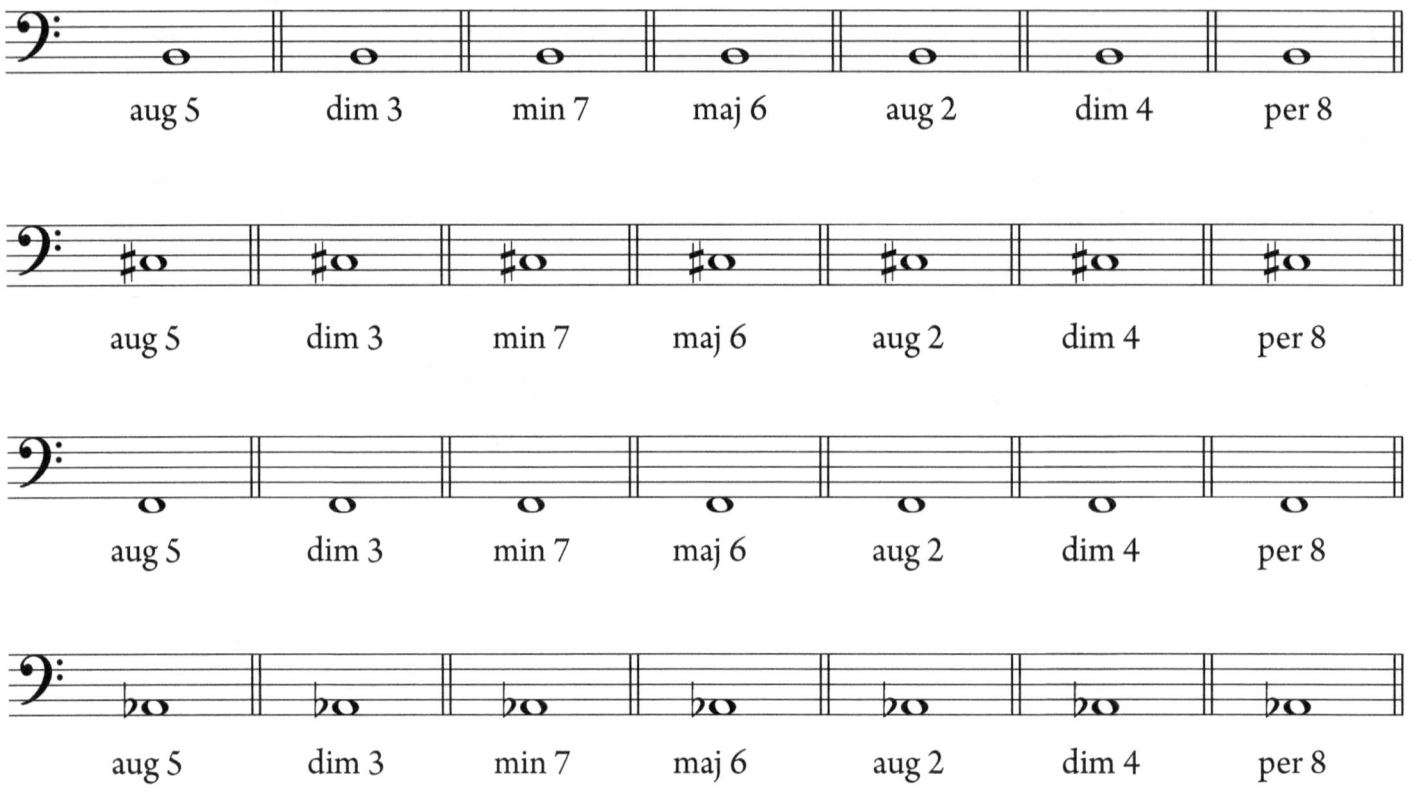

5. Learn the following Italian terms and their translations or definitions.

accelerando, accel.	becoming quicker
a tempo	return to the previous tempo
alla, all'	in the manner of
assai	much, very much (for example, *allegro assai*: very fast)
ben, bene	well
coll', colle, col, colla	with
coll'ottava	with an added octave
con moto	with movement

Intervals Below a Note

So far, we have written intervals above a given note. Intervals can also be written below a given note.

To write intervals below given note, follow these three steps:

1. Determine the bottom note of the interval by counting down the required number of notes from the given note. In the example below, the given note is G and the requested interval is an augmented fourth. Counting down four notes from G, we get D.

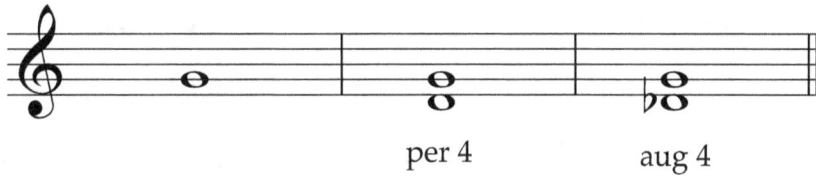

2. Identify the interval using the *bottom* note as the tonic. In the example, D to G is a perfect 4th.

3. Adjust the *bottom* note to obtain the required interval. In the example, D is lowered to D flat to change the interval from a perfect 4th to an augmented 4th.

Here is another example: write a minor 3rd below C sharp.

1. Count down three notes from C sharp (A).

2. Name the resulting interval (major 3rd).

3. Adjust the bottom note to obtain the required interval (change A to A sharp to change the interval from a major 3rd to a minor 3rd).

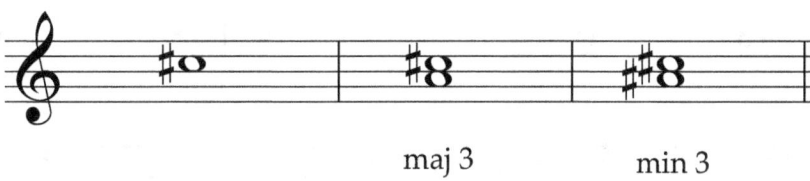

Checklist

Here is a handy checklist for adjusting intervals below a given note:

1. To make a *major* interval *minor*... *raise* the bottom note one half step.
2. To make a *major* interval *diminished*... *raise* the bottom note two half steps.
3. To make a *perfect* interval *diminished*... *raise* the bottom note one half step.
4. To make a *major* or *perfect* interval *augmented*... *lower* the bottom note one half step.

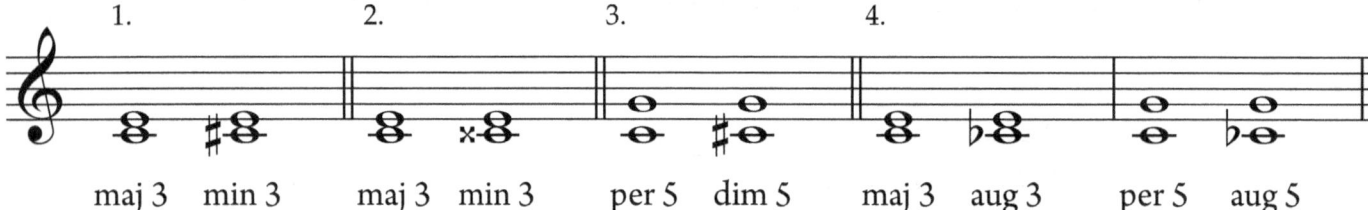

Always identify an interval using the lowest note as the tonic. This applies to melodic intervals, even when the lower note comes after the upper note.

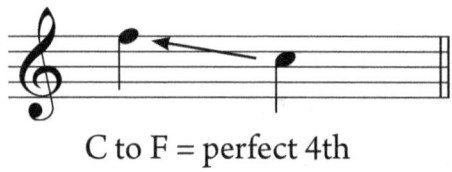

C to F = perfect 4th

1. Write the following intervals below the given notes.

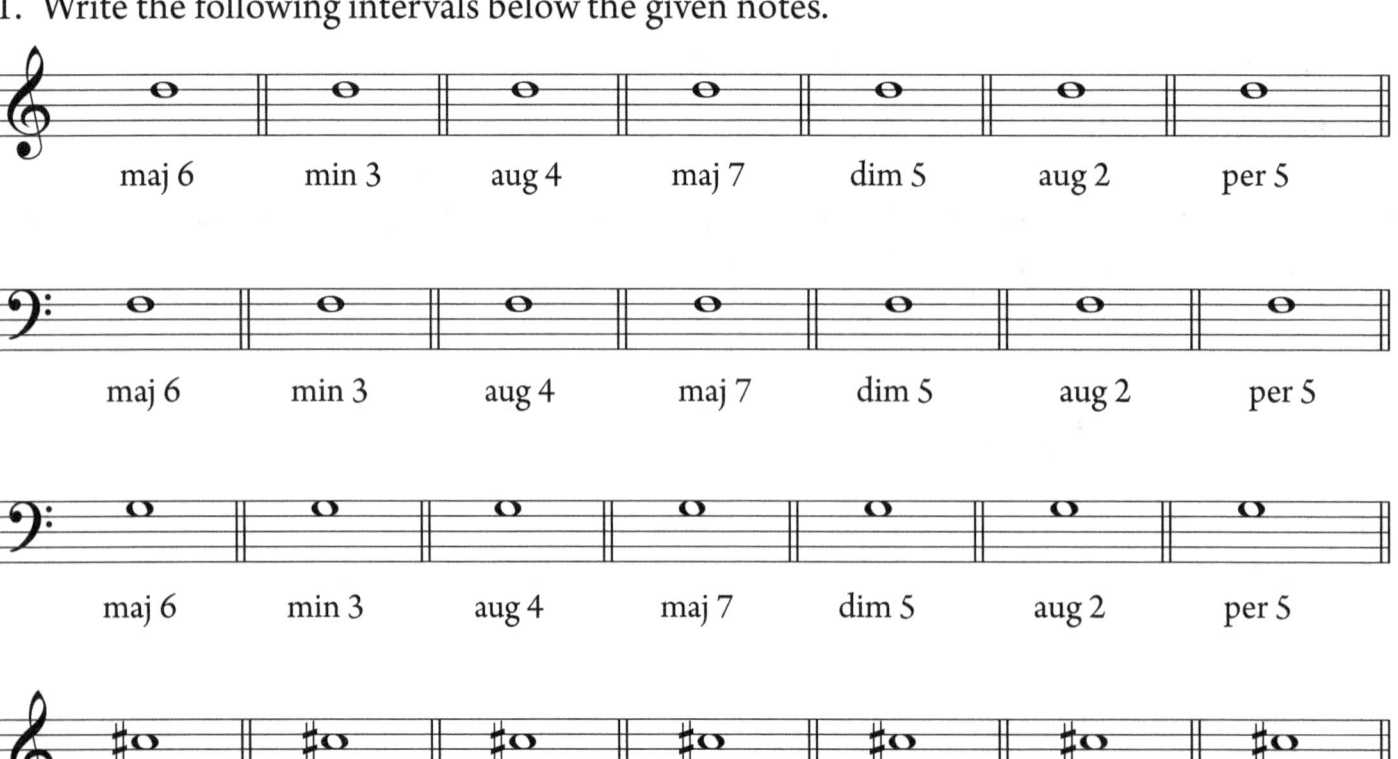

Review One

1. Fill in the blanks.

Major Key	Key signature	Relative minor key
C# major	_____	_____
G♭ major	_____	_____
F# major	_____	_____
B major	_____	_____
D♭ major	_____	_____
C♭ major	_____	_____

2. Write the following key signatures.

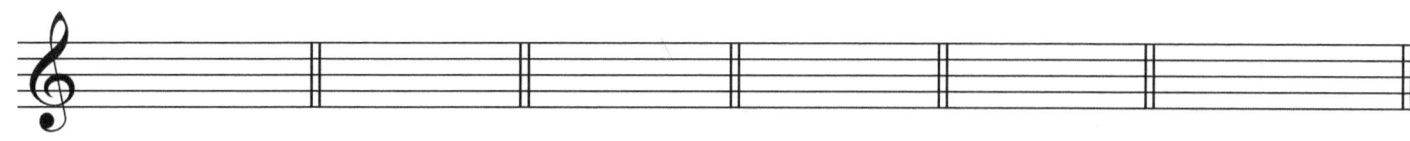

D# minor — B minor — A# minor — E♭ minor — G# minor — A♭ minor

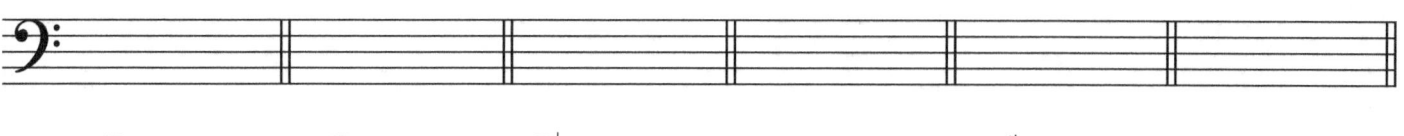

E minor — G minor — B♭ minor — F minor — C# minor — C minor

3. Write the following notes using key signatures.

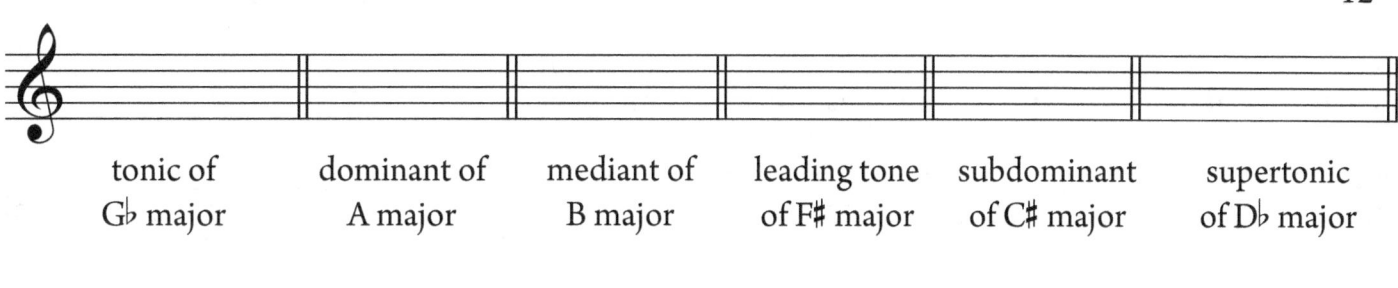

tonic of G♭ major — dominant of A major — mediant of B major — leading tone of F# major — subdominant of C# major — supertonic of D♭ major

tonic of C♭ major — submediant of A minor — leading tone of C# minor — dominant of E♭ minor — supertonic of A# minor — subdominant of G minor

4. Write the following scales in half notes, ascending and descending, using key signatures.

The major scale with C# as the supertonic

The major scale with the key signature of six flats

The harmonic minor scale with A# as the dominant

The melodic minor scale with the key signature of five flats

The major scale with B♭ as the leading tone

The harmonic minor scale with A♭ as the tonic

The melodic minor scale with the key signature of three sharps

The major scale with B♭ as the subdominant

5. Name the following intervals. Invert them and name the inversions.

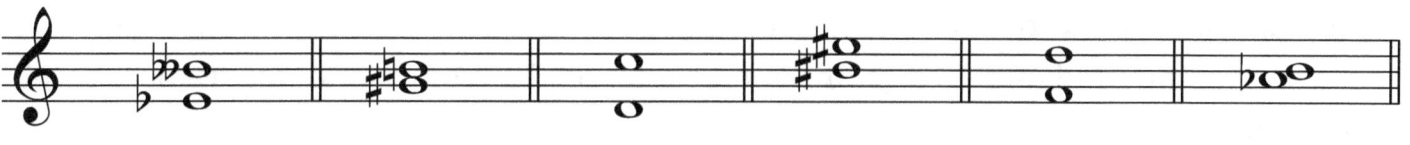

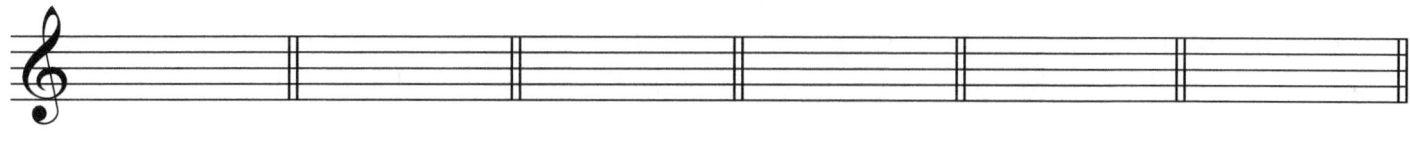

6. Match the following terms with their definitions.

tranquillo	___	(a) in the manner of
animato	___	(b) light, nimble, quick
ben	___	(c) with movement
leggiero	___	(d) return to the previous tempo
espressivo	___	(e) brilliant
con brio	___	(f) lively, animated
con moto	___	(g) with
assai	___	(h) quiet, tranquil
con espressione	___	(i) well
col, colle	___	(j) becoming quicker
alla	___	(k) with an added octave
brillante	___	(l) with expression
accelerando	___	(m) much, very much
coll' ottava	___	(n) with vigour, spirit
a tempo	___	(o) expressive, with expression
con	___	(p) with

Time

In **compound time**, the basic beat is a dotted note. Time signatures in compound time have 6 (compound duple), 9 (compound triple), or 12 (compound quadruple), as the upper number.

In **compound duple time**, there are two beats in each measure. A beat is a group of three pulses and is represented by a dotted note. The upper number of the time signature is always 6, which indicates that each measure contains six pulses (two beats of three pulses). The lower number, which indicates the note that receives one pulse, can be 4, 8, or 16.

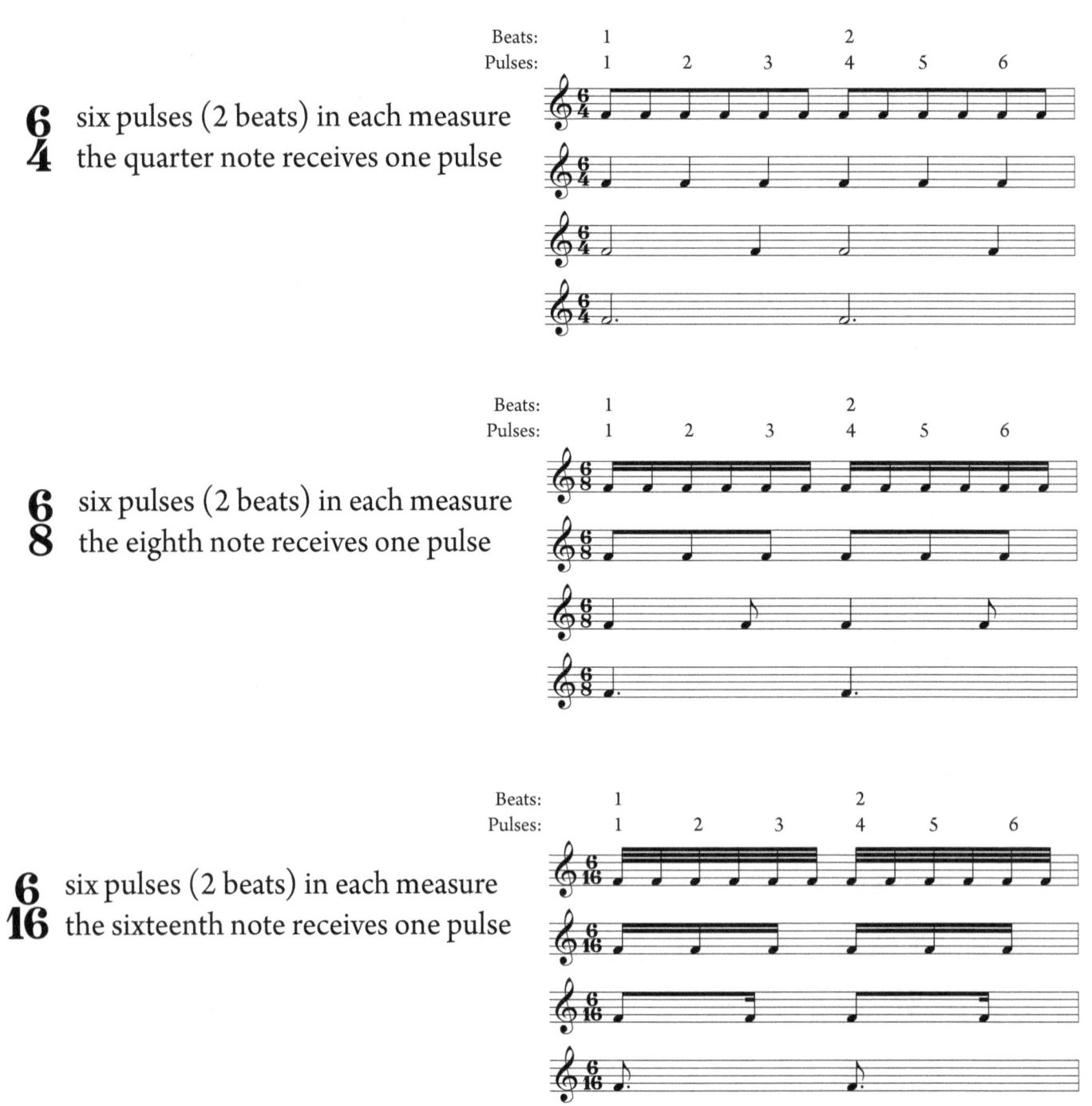

6/4 six pulses (2 beats) in each measure
the quarter note receives one pulse

6/8 six pulses (2 beats) in each measure
the eighth note receives one pulse

6/16 six pulses (2 beats) in each measure
the sixteenth note receives one pulse

In **compound triple time**, there are three beats in each measure. The upper number of the time signature is always 9, which indicates that each measure contains nine pulses (three beats of three pulses). The lower number, which indicates the note that receives one pulse, can be 4, 8, or 16.

9/4 nine pulses (3 beats) in each measure
the quarter note receives one pulse

9/8 nine pulses (3 beats) in each measure
the eighth note receives one pulse

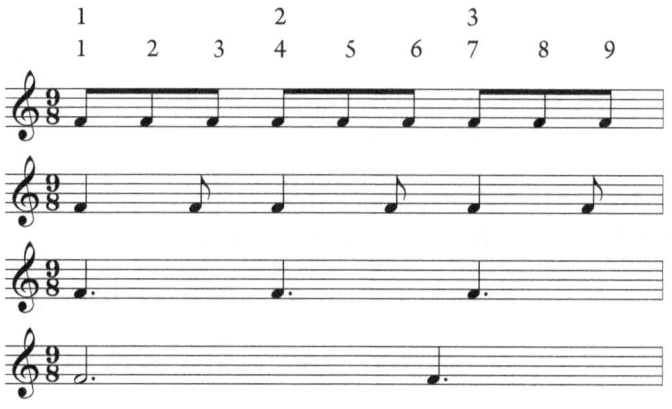

9/16 nine pulses (3 beats) in each measure
the sixteenth note receives one pulse

In **compound quadruple time**, there are four beats in each measure. The upper number of the time signature is always 12, which indicates that each measure contains twelve pulses (four beats of three pulses). The lower number, which indicates the note that receives one pulse, can be 4, 8, or 16.

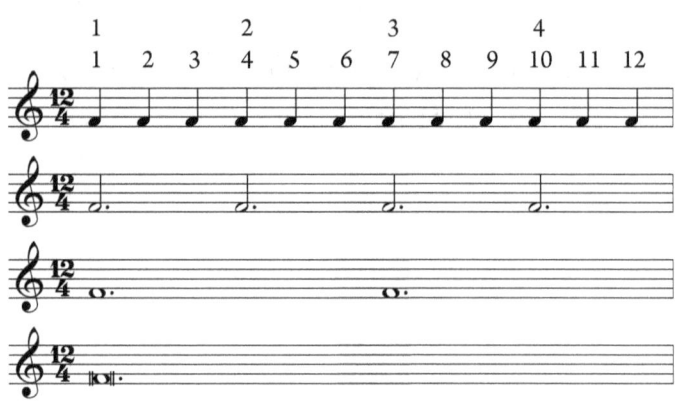

12 twelve pulses (4 beats) in each measure
4 the quarter note receives one pulse

12 twelve pulses (4 beats) in each measure
8 the eighth note receives one pulse

12 twelve pulses (4 beats) in each measure
16 the sixteenth note receives one pulse

1. Add time signatures to the following one measure rhythms. Circle each beat (group of three pulses).

2. Add bar lines to the following melodies.

Rests

In compound time, as in simple time, a whole rest is used to indicate an entire measure of silence in any time signature.

Remember that notes are grouped in three pulse patterns in compound time. Rests must also follow this three pulse pattern.

When adding rests to complete the *first two pulses* of a three pulse group in compound time, *use one rest*.

When adding rests to complete the *last two pulses* of a three pulse group in compound time, *use two rests*.

In compound triple time, you may *join beats 1 and 2*, but *do not join beats 2 and 3*.

In compound quadruple time, you may *complete the first or last half of the bar with one dotted rest. Do not join beats 2 and 3 into one rest.*

Correct   Correct   Correct   Incorrect

1. Add rests under the brackets according to the time signatures.

Simple time signatures divide the beat into two equal parts. Compound time signatures divide the beat into three equal parts.

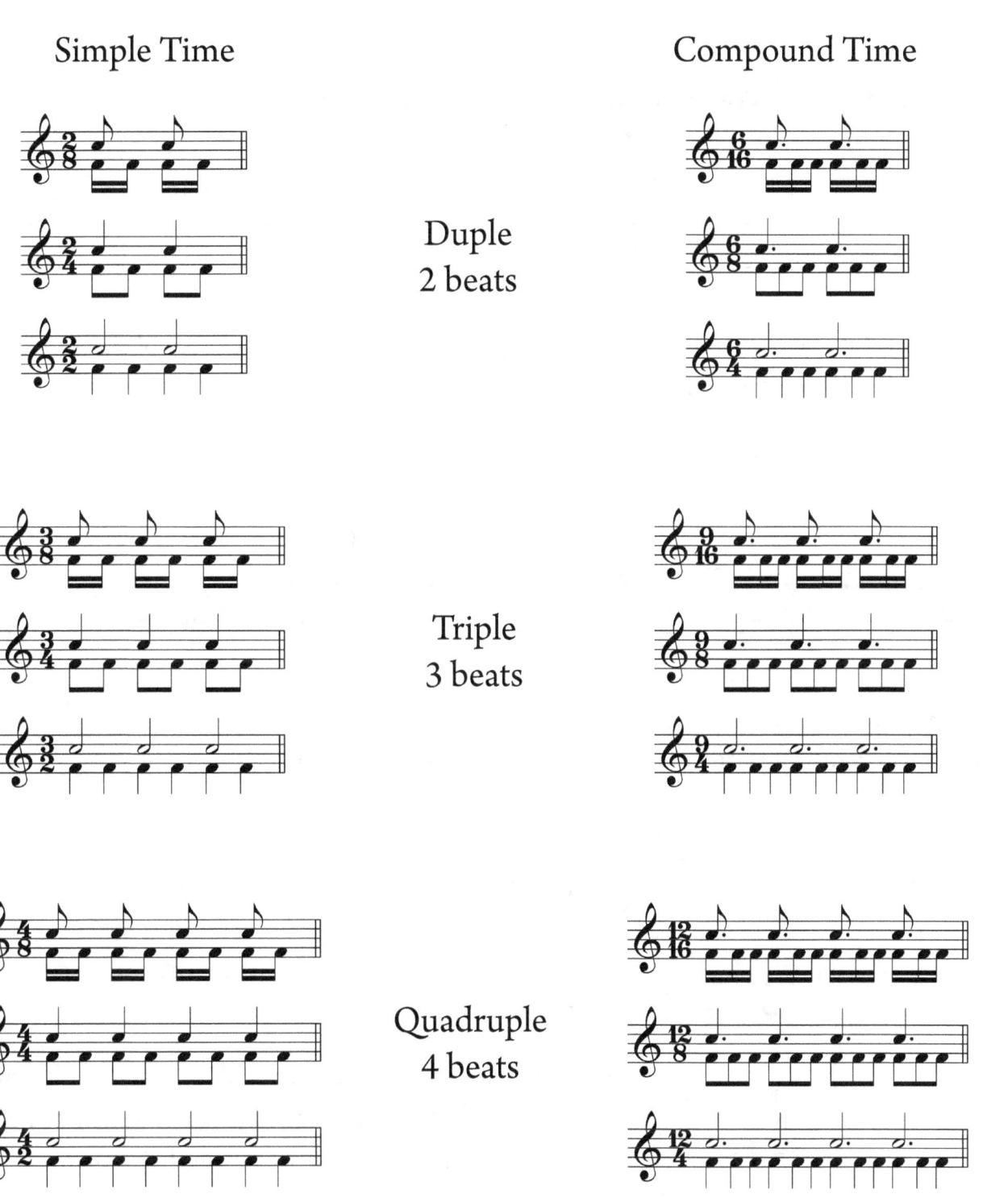

The **thirty second** and **sixty fourth** notes and rests are written as follows:

4 thirty second notes   =   2 sixteenth notes = 1 eighth note

Triplets

A triplet is a group of three notes that are played in the time of two notes of the same value. They are most frequently found in simple time.

Triplets are usually indicated by a "3". Here are some examples of different ways triplets can be written.

Here are some examples of the different ways triplets can be used:

The *three* eighth notes played in the time of *two* eighth notes equal one beat.

Three sixteenth notes played in the time of *two* sixteenth notes equal one half beat.

This triplet has only two notes. Together, the quarter and the eighth notes are equal to *three* eighth notes but they are played in the time of *two* eighth notes.

This triplet has a dotted rhythm. Once again, the three note rhythm is equal to *three* eighth notes that are played in the time of *two* eighth notes.

Double Dots

A second dot after a note is worth half the value of the first dot.

1. Add time signatures to the following one measure rhythms in simple or compound time.

Irregular Groups

A **duplet** is a group of *two* notes that are played in the time of *three* notes of the same value. Duplets are found in *compound time.*

A **quadruplet** is a group of *four* notes that are played in the time of *three* notes of the same value. Quadruplets are found in *compound time.*

A **quintuplet** is a group of *five* notes that are played in the time of *three, four or six* notes of the same value, depending on the time signature.

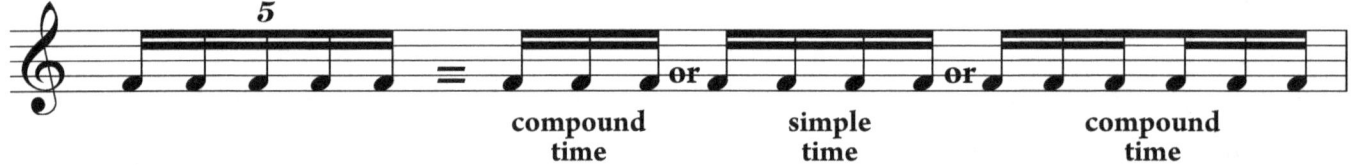

A **sextuplet** is a group of *six* notes that are played in the time of *three or four* notes of the same value, depending on the time signature.

A **septuplet** is a group of *seven* notes that are played in the time of *three or four* notes of the same value, depending on the time signature.

To determine the value of an irregular group of notes, examine the remaining beats, (and partial beats) in the measure. The irregular group will fill the remaining beats (or partial beats) required to complete the measure.

1. Add bar lines to the following melodies according to the time signatures.

2. Add rests under the brackets according to the time signatures.

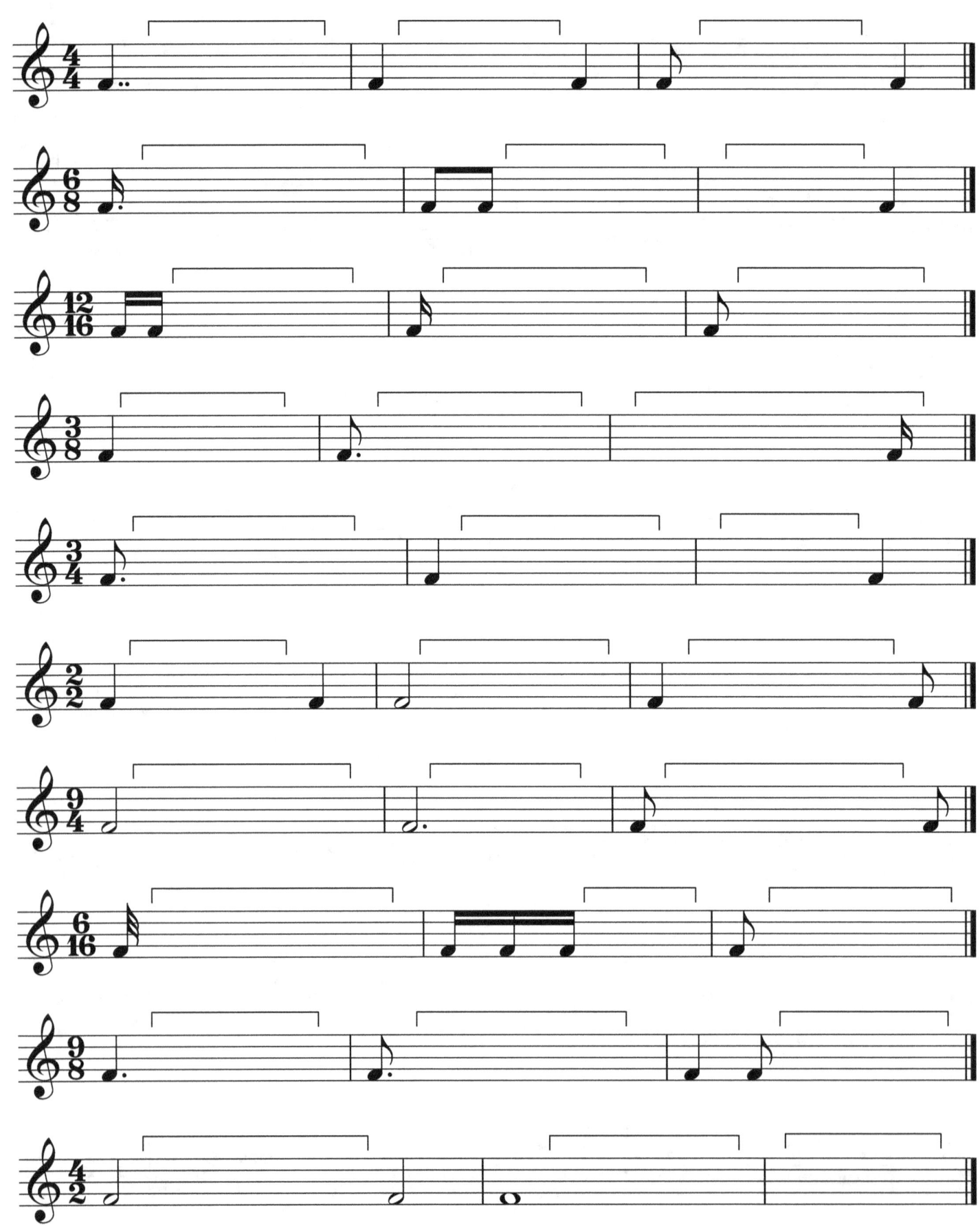

Syncopation

Syncopation occurs when the pattern of strong and weak beats in a measure is altered, and the accent is shifted from the strong beat to the weak beat.

3. Write three measure rhythms for the following time signatures. Use a different rhythm for each measure.

4. Add time signatures to the following one measure rhythms.

5. Add rests under the brackets according to the time signatures.

6. Add stems to the following noteheads, and group them to create one measure rhythms according to the time signatures.

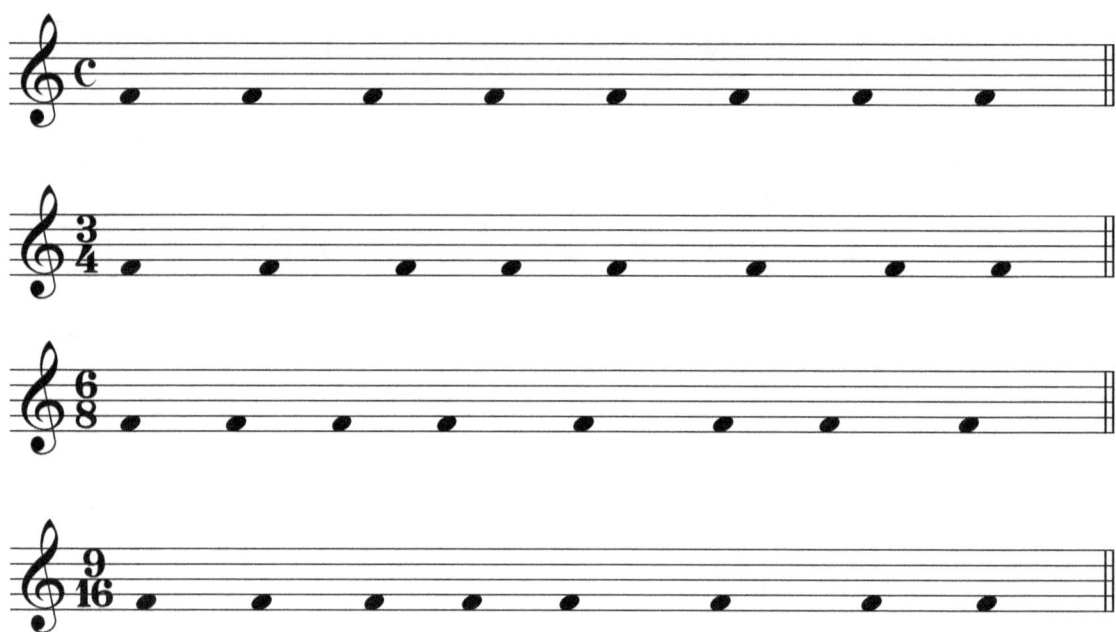

7. Learn the following Italian terms and their definitions.

non	not
non troppo	not too much
ottava, 8va	the interval of an octave
piu	more
piu mosso	more movement (quicker)
poco	little
poco a poco	little by little
quasi	almost, as if
sempre	always, continuously

Review Two

1. The following scales start on degrees other than the tonic. For each scale:
   (a) name the key and type of scale (major, harmonic or melodic minor)
   (b) name the degree of the scale on which the scale begins

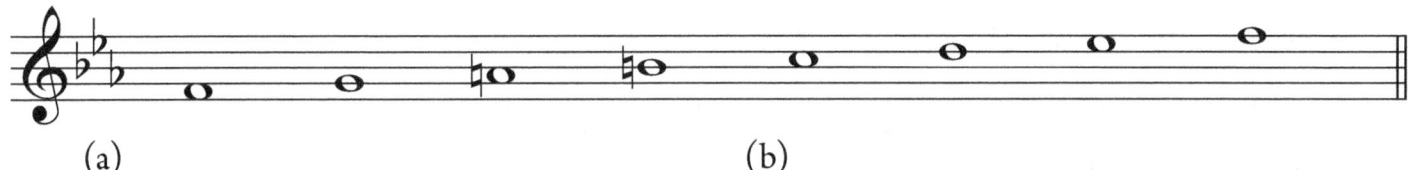

(a) _____ (b) _____

(a) _____ (b) _____

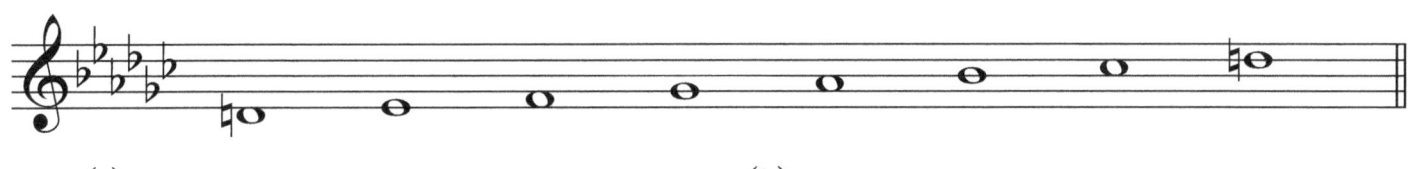

(a) _____ (b) _____

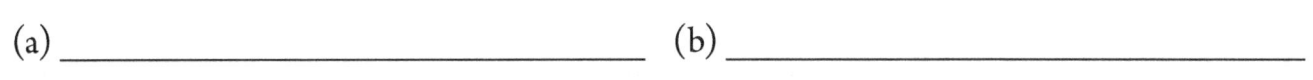

(a) _____ (b) _____

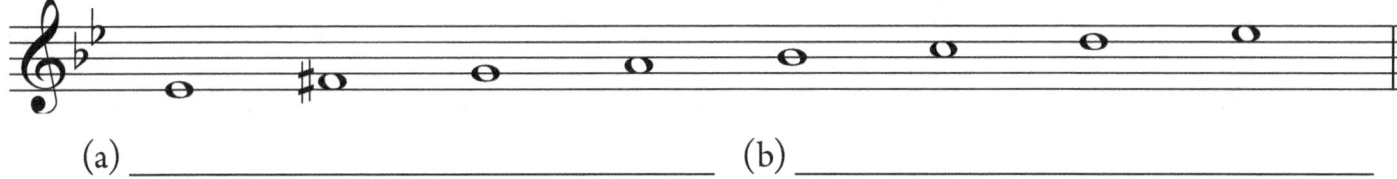

(a) _____ (b) _____

2. Define the following Italian terms.

   accelerando _____

   con moto _____

   assai _____

   non troppo _____

   sempre _____

3. Write the following intervals using F sharp as the lowest note for each.   10

maj 6   min 3   per 5   aug 2   dim 4

4. Invert the above intervals and name the inversions.   10

5. Write the following notes using key signatures.   20

supertonic of   dominant of   leading tone of   mediant of   subdominant of
F♯ major   A major   D minor   E♭ major   D♭ major

submediant of   tonic of   dominant of   supertonic of   leading tone of
B minor   B major   C♯ minor   F minor   E minor

6. Name the relative major of the following minor keys.   10

D minor _____   C minor _____

C♯ minor _____   B minor _____

G minor _____   F♯ minor _____

E♭ minor _____   F minor _____

A♭ minor _____   B♭ minor _____

7. Complete the following measures by adding rests under the brackets.

8. Add time signatures to the following rhythms.

Chords

A **triad** is a three note chord. The three notes of a triad are called the **root**, the **third** and the **fifth**.

A **major triad** consists of the intervals of a **major 3rd** and a **perfect 5th** above the root. In the F major triad below, F to A is a major 3rd and F to C is a perfect 5th.

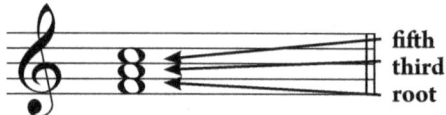

A **minor triad** consists of the intervals of a **minor 3rd** and a **perfect 5th** above the root. In the F major triad below, F to A♭ is a minor 3rd and F to C is a perfect 5th.

Triads can be written and played in two ways:

1. **Solid (blocked)** all three notes are written, or sound at the same time.
2. **Broken** each note is written, or is played, one after the other.

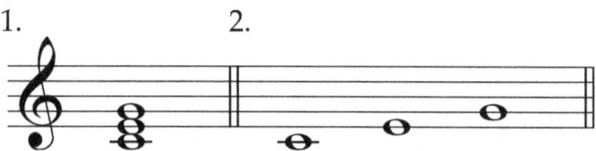

Triads can occur in three different positions:

1. If the *root* of the chord is the lowest note, the triad is in *root position*.
2. Is the *third* of the chord is the lowest note, the triad is in *first inversion*.
3. If the *fifth* of the chord is the lowest note, the triad is in *second inversion*.

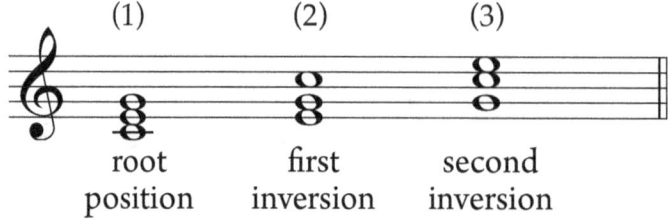

The inversions of a triad are created by raising the bottom note one octave. In the example above, moving C up one octave from route position creates the first inversion. Moving E up one octave from the first inversion creates the second inversion.

1. Identify the following triads as a major (maj) or minor (min).

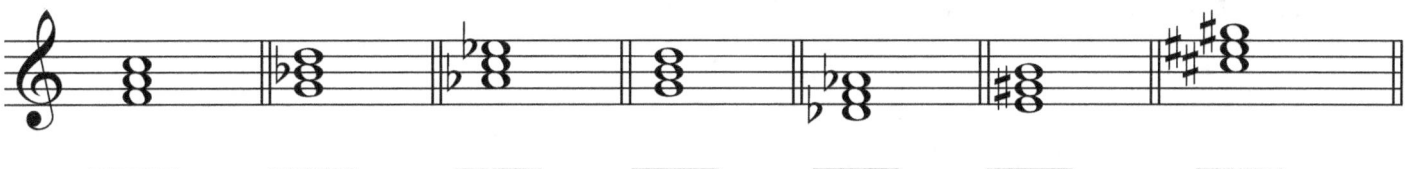

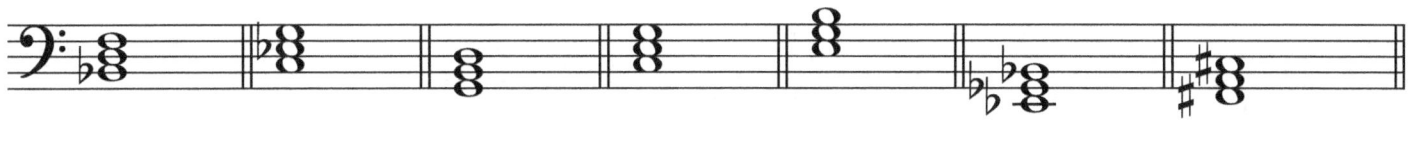

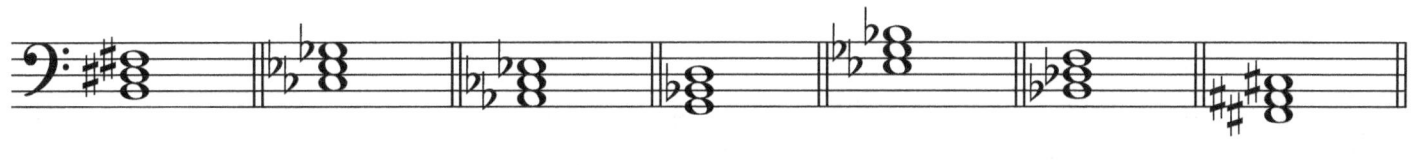

2. Write major triads in root position above the given notes. In the measures that follow, write to the triads in first and second inversion.

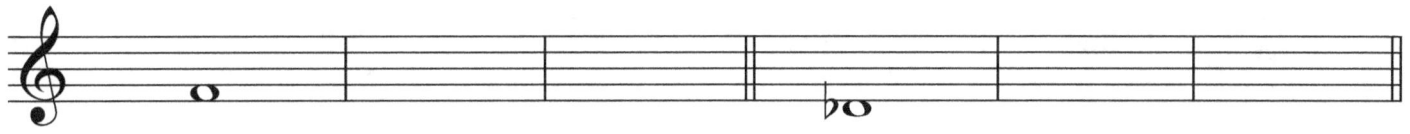

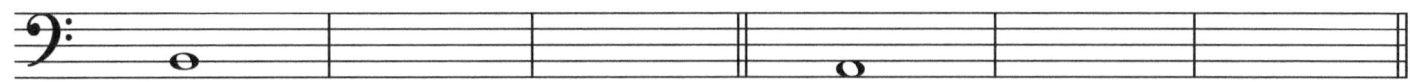

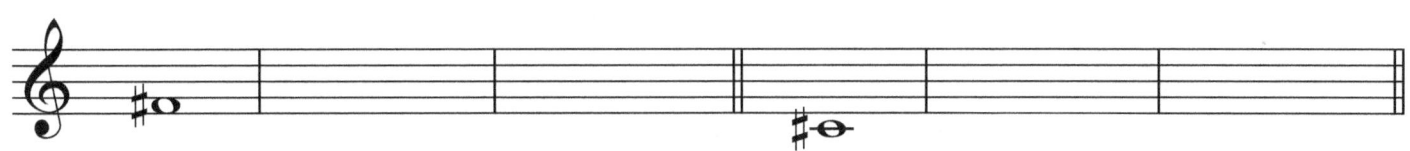

3. Write minor triads in root position above the given notes. In the measures that follow, write to the triads in first and second inversion.

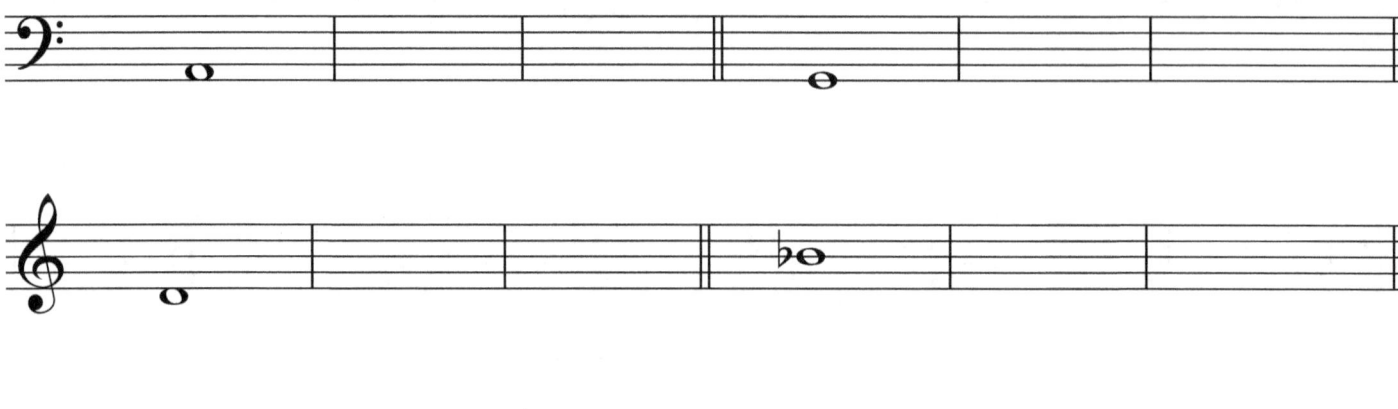

4. Name the roots of the following triads.

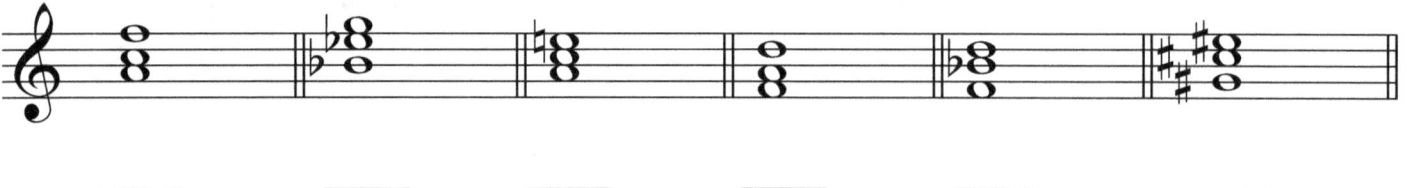

___   ___   ___   ___   ___   ___

___   ___   ___   ___   ___   ___

You may be asked to identify a given triad. Here are three steps to determine the root, the type, and the position of the triad.

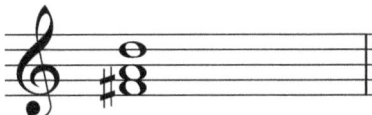

1. Put the triad in root position. In other words, rearrange the notes so that they are a 3rd apart. In root position, the bottom note of the triad is the root. **In the example below, the bottom note D is the root.**

2. Identify the intervals between the root and the third, and between the root and the fifth. This will tell you the type of triad (major or minor). **In the example below, the triad consists of a major 3rd and a perfect 5th. Therefore it is a major triad.**

3. Look at the lowest note of the given triad. If this note is the root, the triad is in root position. If it is the third, the triad in first inversion. If it is the fifth, the triad is in second inversion. **In the given triad, the lowest note F sharp is the third of the triad. Therefore, this triad is in first inversion.**

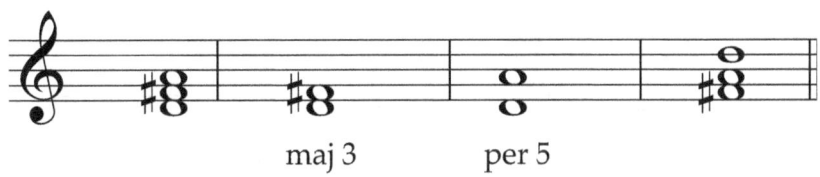

5. Name the root, type, and position of the following triads.

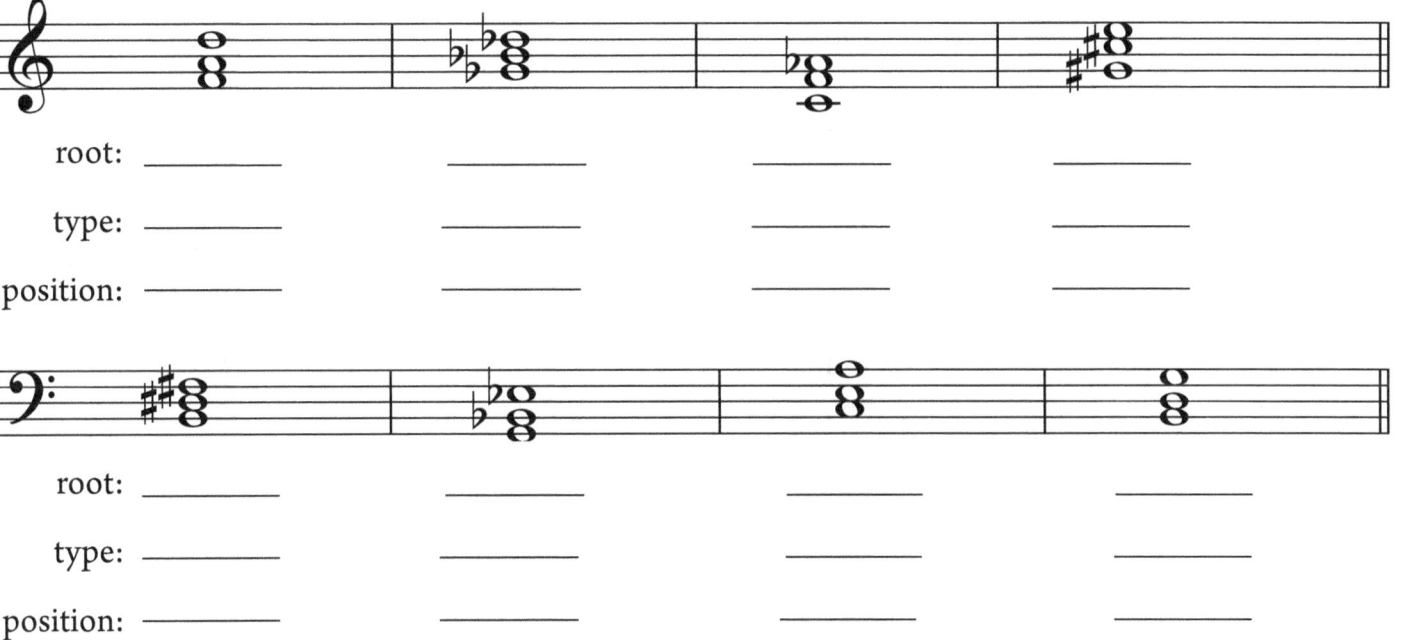

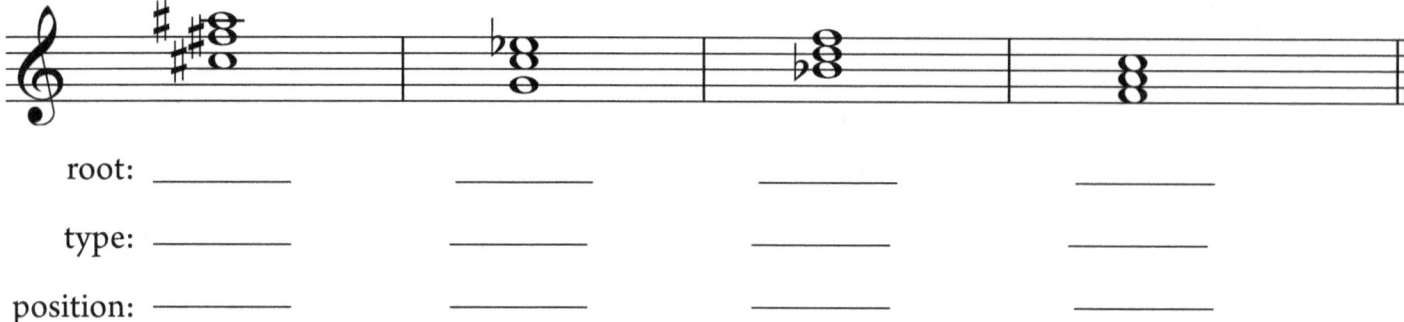

root: _____   _____   _____   _____

type: _____   _____   _____   _____

position: _____   _____   _____   _____

6. Write the following triads in root position, using accidentals instead of a key signature.

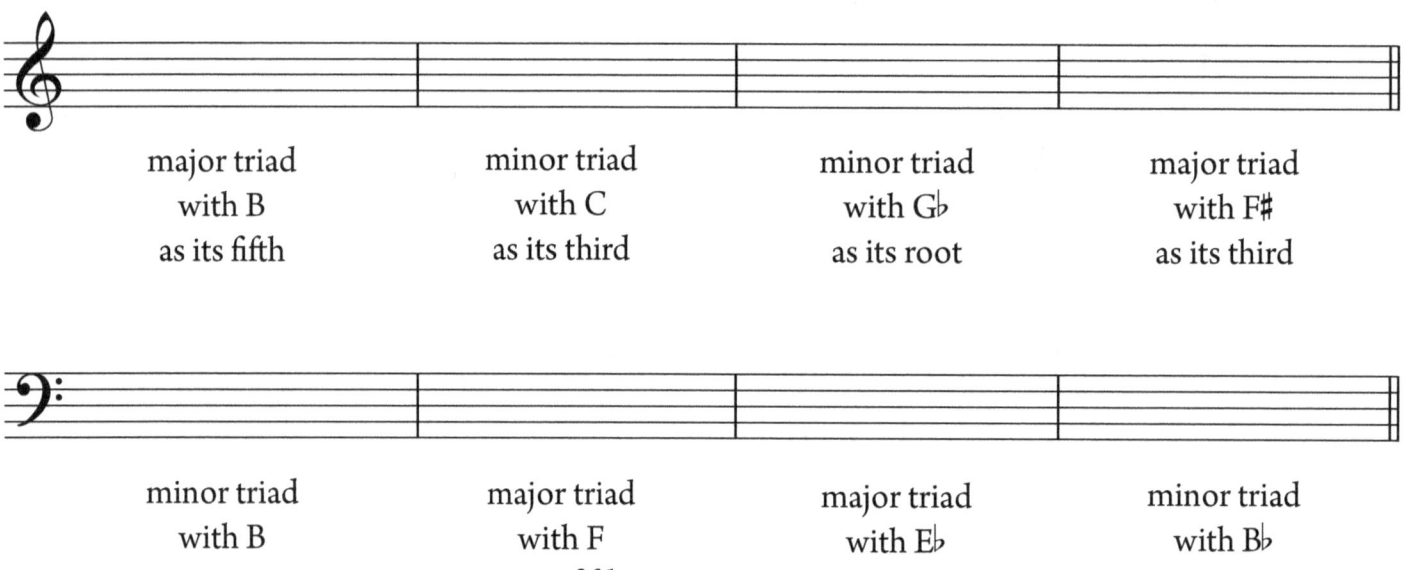

major triad with B as its fifth | minor triad with C as its third | minor triad with G♭ as its root | major triad with F♯ as its third

minor triad with B as its root | major triad with F as its fifth | major triad with E♭ as its third | minor triad with B♭ as its root

7. Write the following triads using accidentals instead of a key signature.

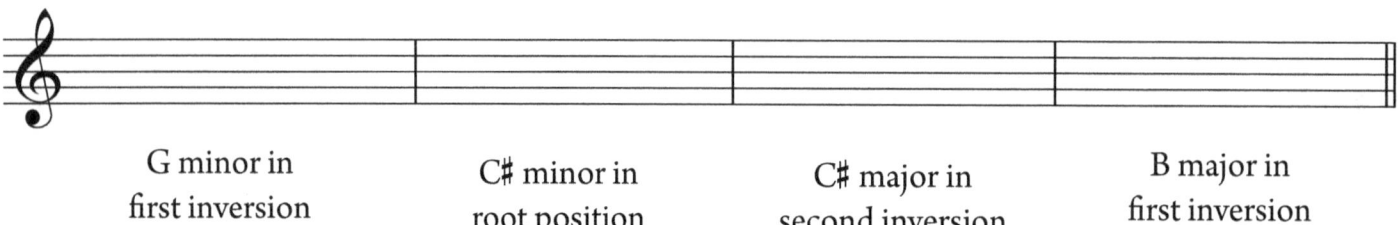

G minor in first inversion | C♯ minor in root position | C♯ major in second inversion | B major in first inversion

Triads can be built on any degree of the major or minor scale.

These are the major and minor triads that occur in the major scale. From the example below in C Major, we see that major triads occur on I, IV, and V. Minor triads occur on ii, iii, and vi. We use uppercase Roman numerals to indicate scale degrees with major triads and lowercase numerals to indicate scale degrees with minor triads.

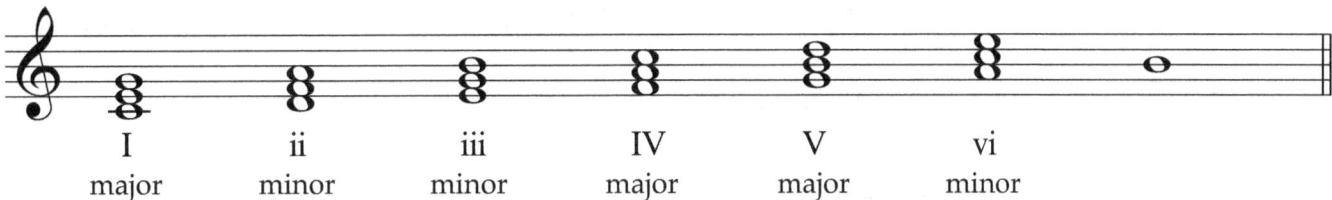

In a minor key, major triads occur on V and VI, and minor triads occur on i and iv. Study the example below, in which triads are built on the degrees of the A harmonic minor scale.

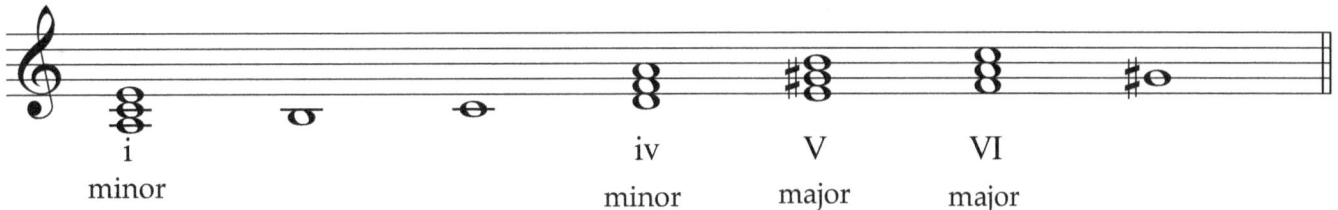

Triads take the same name as the scale degrees that they are built upon. For example, a triad built on the third note of the C major scale is called the *mediant triad of C major*. A triad built on the fifth note of the A minor scale is called the *dominant triad of A minor*.

1. Using key signatures, write root position tonic, subdominant, and dominant triads in the following keys.

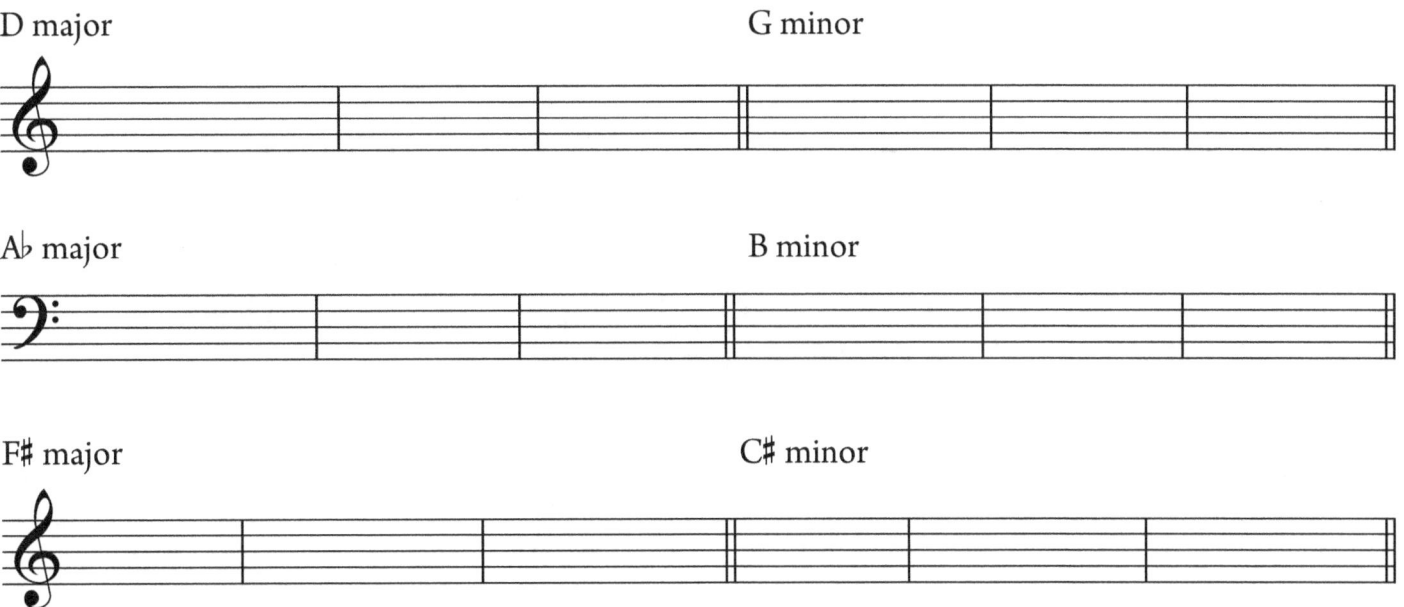

2. Write the following triads, using a key signature for each.

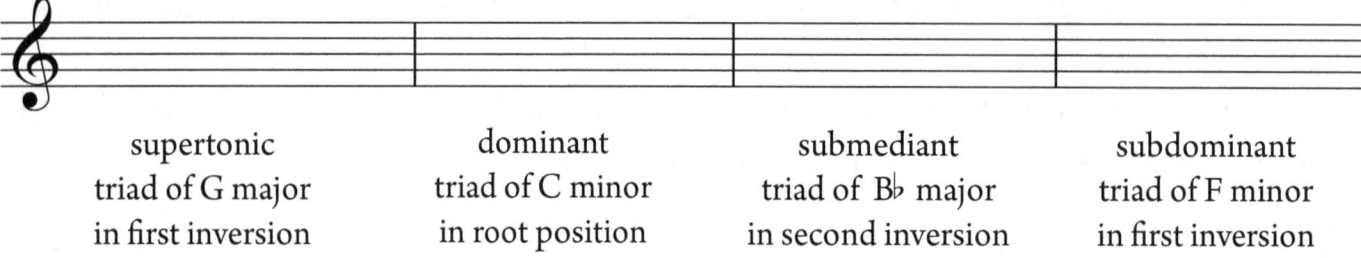

supertonic	dominant	submediant	subdominant
triad of G major	triad of C minor	triad of B♭ major	triad of F minor
in first inversion	in root position	in second inversion	in first inversion

3. Write the following triads, using accidentals instead of a key signature.

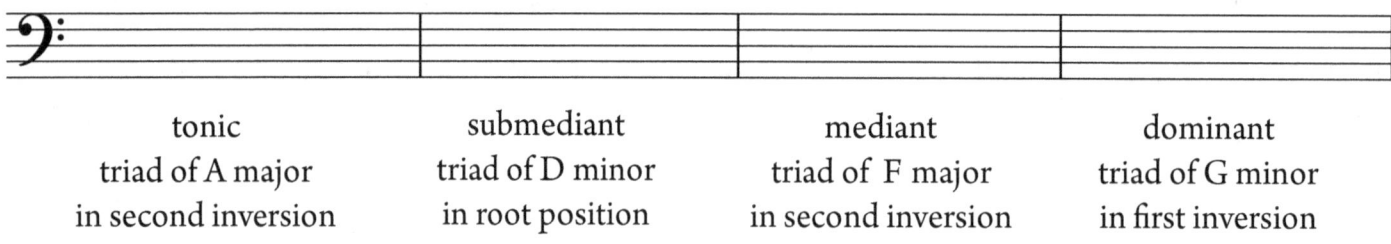

tonic	submediant	mediant	dominant
triad of A major	triad of D minor	triad of F major	triad of G minor
in second inversion	in root position	in second inversion	in first inversion

4. Names of root, type, and position of the following chords. Then name of the major key in which each triad can be found and name the scale degree on which each is built.

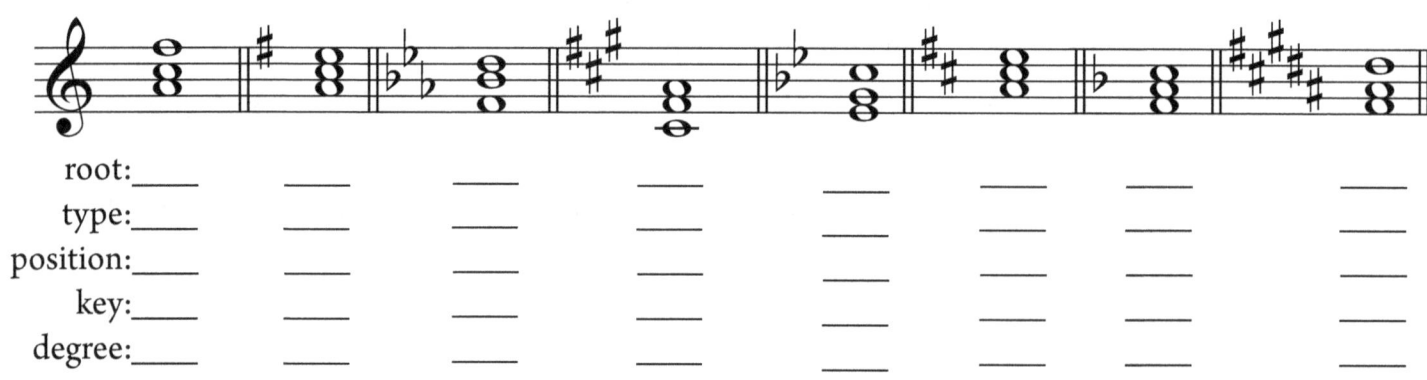

root: ____ ____ ____ ____ ____ ____ ____ ____
type: ____ ____ ____ ____ ____ ____ ____ ____
position: ____ ____ ____ ____ ____ ____ ____ ____
key: ____ ____ ____ ____ ____ ____ ____ ____
degree: ____ ____ ____ ____ ____ ____ ____ ____

5. Names of root, type, and position of the following chords. Then name of the minor key in which each triad can be found and name the scale degree on which each is built.

root: ____ ____ ____ ____ ____ ____ ____ ____
type: ____ ____ ____ ____ ____ ____ ____ ____
position: ____ ____ ____ ____ ____ ____ ____ ____
key: ____ ____ ____ ____ ____ ____ ____ ____
degree: ____ ____ ____ ____ ____ ____ ____ ____

Close and Open Position

So far, we have written and identified triads in **close position**. When a triad is in close position, the three notes of the triad are as close together as possible.

Triads can also be written in **open position**. In open position, the notes are spread over an octave or over one or two staves. The C major triads in the example below are all in open position. One of the notes (usually the root) can be doubled.

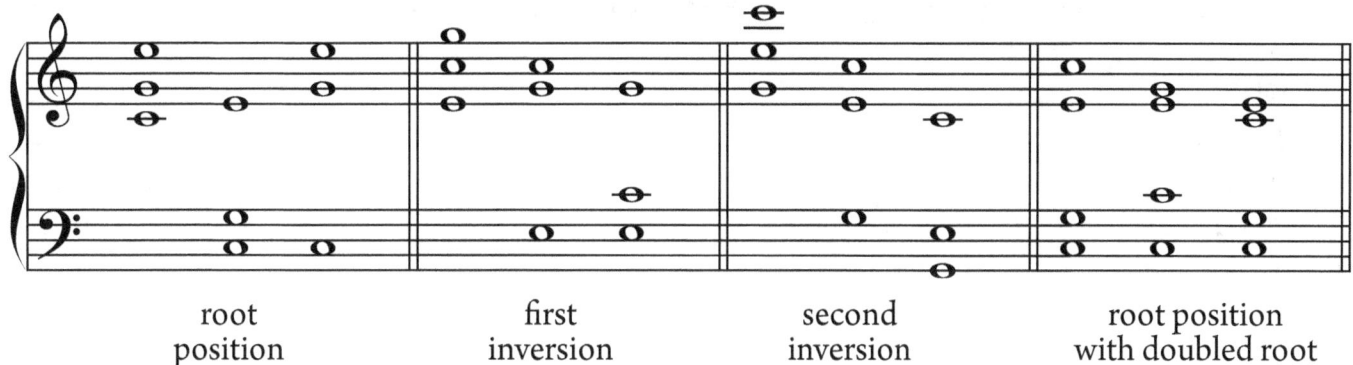

Remember that the lowest note determines the inversion of the triad.

1. If the root is the lowest note, the triad is in root position.
2. If the third is the lowest note, the triad is in first inversion.
3. If the fifth is the lowest note, the triad is in second inversion.

1. Name the root, type, and position of the following chords.

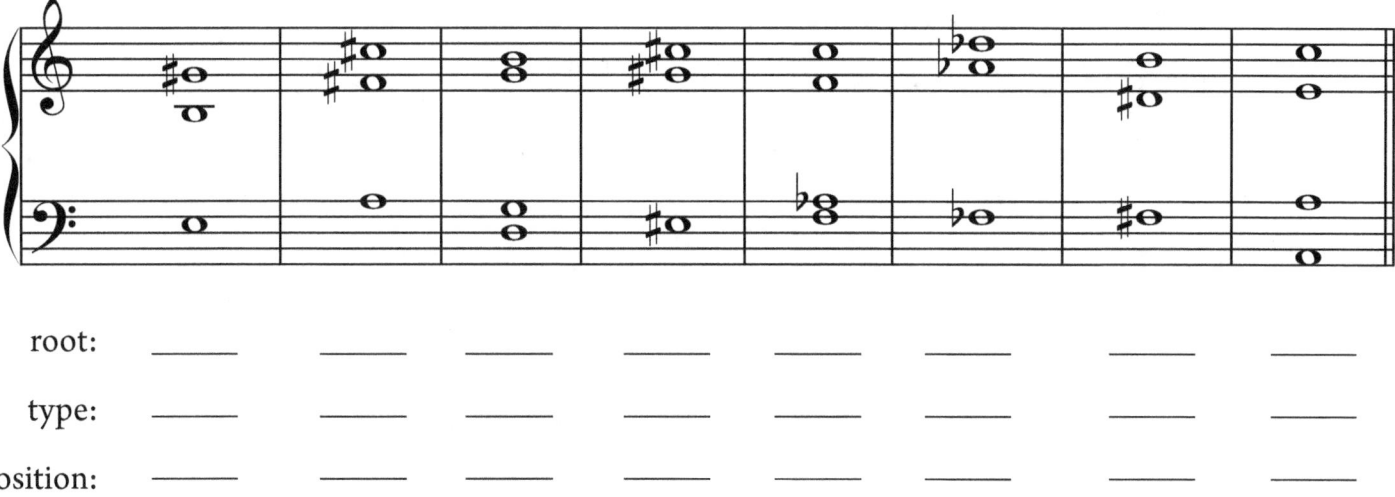

root: _____   _____   _____   _____   _____   _____   _____   _____

type: _____   _____   _____   _____   _____   _____   _____   _____

position: _____   _____   _____   _____   _____   _____   _____   _____

2. Name the root, type, and position of the following chords. Then name the major key in which each triad can be found and name the scale degree on which each is built.

root: ____ ____ ____ ____ ____ ____ ____ ____
type: ____ ____ ____ ____ ____ ____ ____ ____
position: ____ ____ ____ ____ ____ ____ ____ ____
key: ____ ____ ____ ____ ____ ____ ____ ____
degree: ____ ____ ____ ____ ____ ____ ____ ____

3. Learn the following Italian terms and their definitions.

rubato	a flexible tempo, using slight variations of speed to enhance musical expression
senza	without
tenuto	held, sustained
tre corde	three strings; release the left (piano) pedal
troppo	too much
una corde	one string; press the left (piano) pedal
vivace	lively, brisk

Broken Chords in Instrumental Music

The chords we have studied appear frequently in instrumental music. Sometimes they appear in solid (blocked) form, and sometimes they appear in a variety of broken forms. Study the following pieces and a harmonic reduction of the broken chords in the left-hand accompaniment. The following sonatina has a left hand accompaniment consisting of broken triads.

Sonatina, op. 36, no. 1 (2nd movement)

Muzio Clementi

The Kuhlau Sonatina below contains a broken chord pattern in the left-hand called an *Alberti bass*. This is a typical accompaniment pattern from the classical era. The chord in m. 4, a dominant seventh, will be covered in the next lesson.

The left hand accompaniment of the Brahms waltz below uses another broken chord pattern. This is a common accompaniment for a waltz.

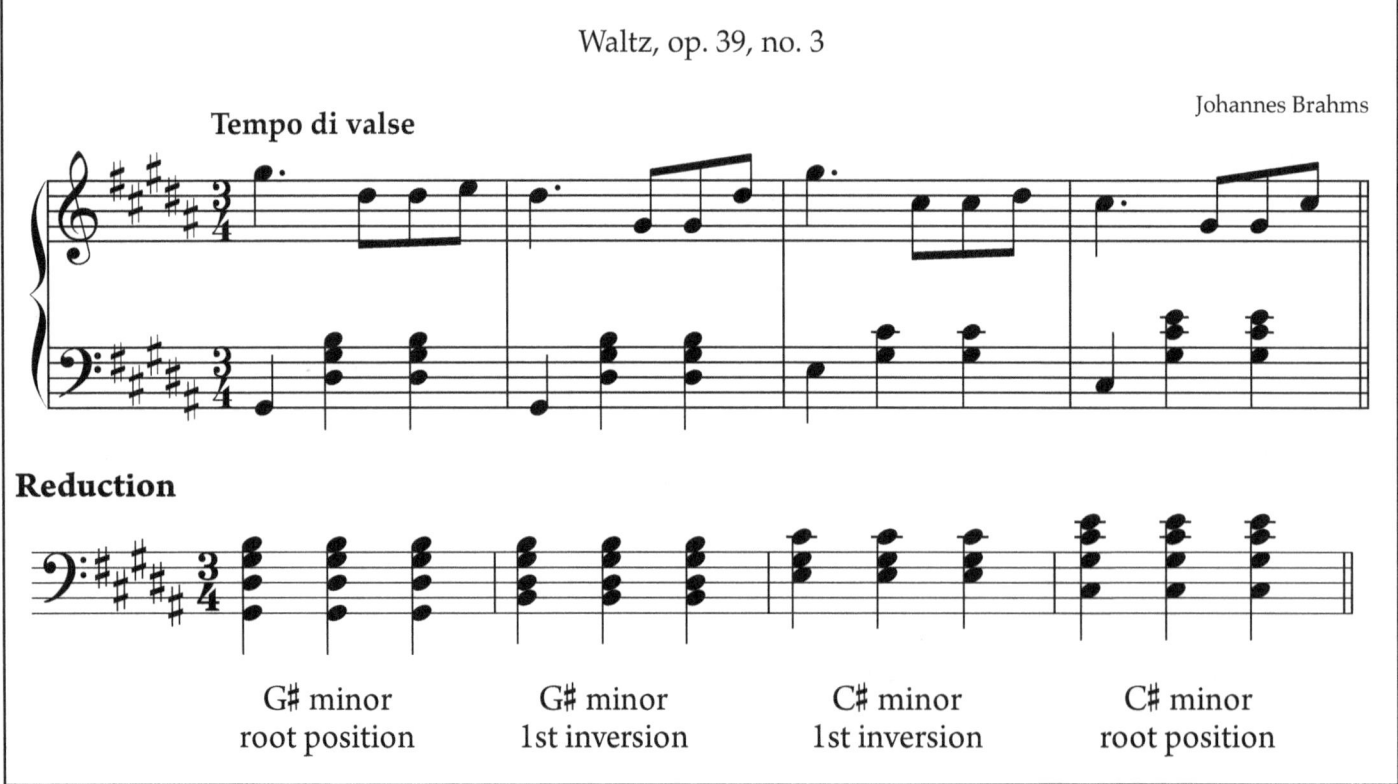

Chopin's *Fantasie- Impromptu* uses an arpeggio accompaniment.

Fantaisie-Impromptu

Frederic Chopin

Reduction

C♯ minor root position	C♯ minor 1st inversion	C♯ minor root position	C♯ minor 1st inversion

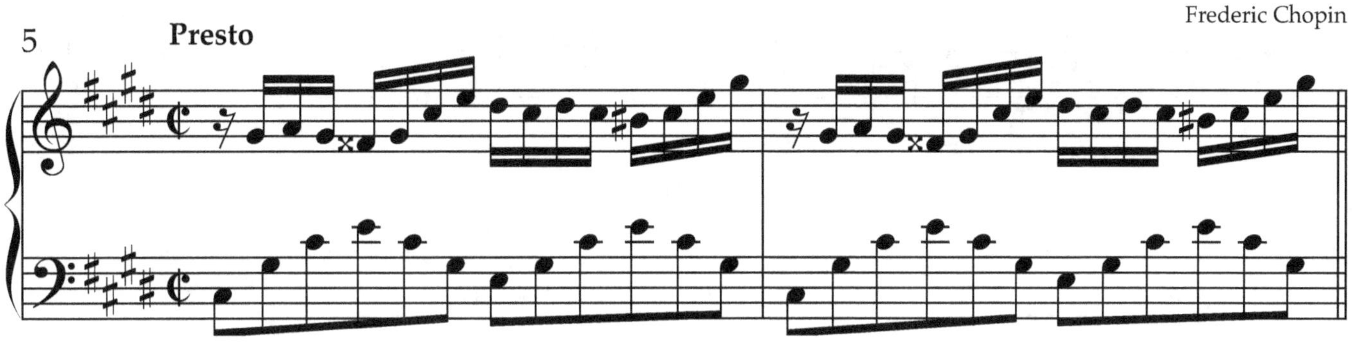

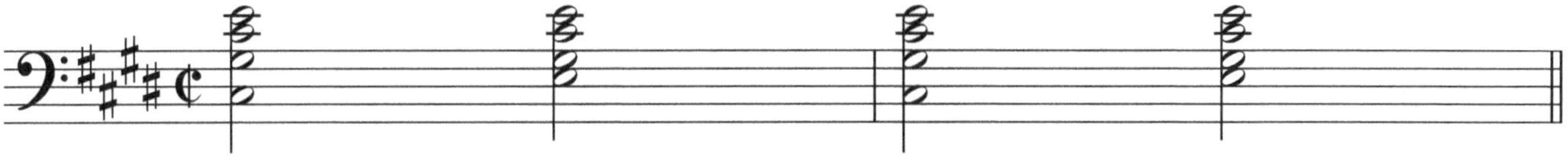

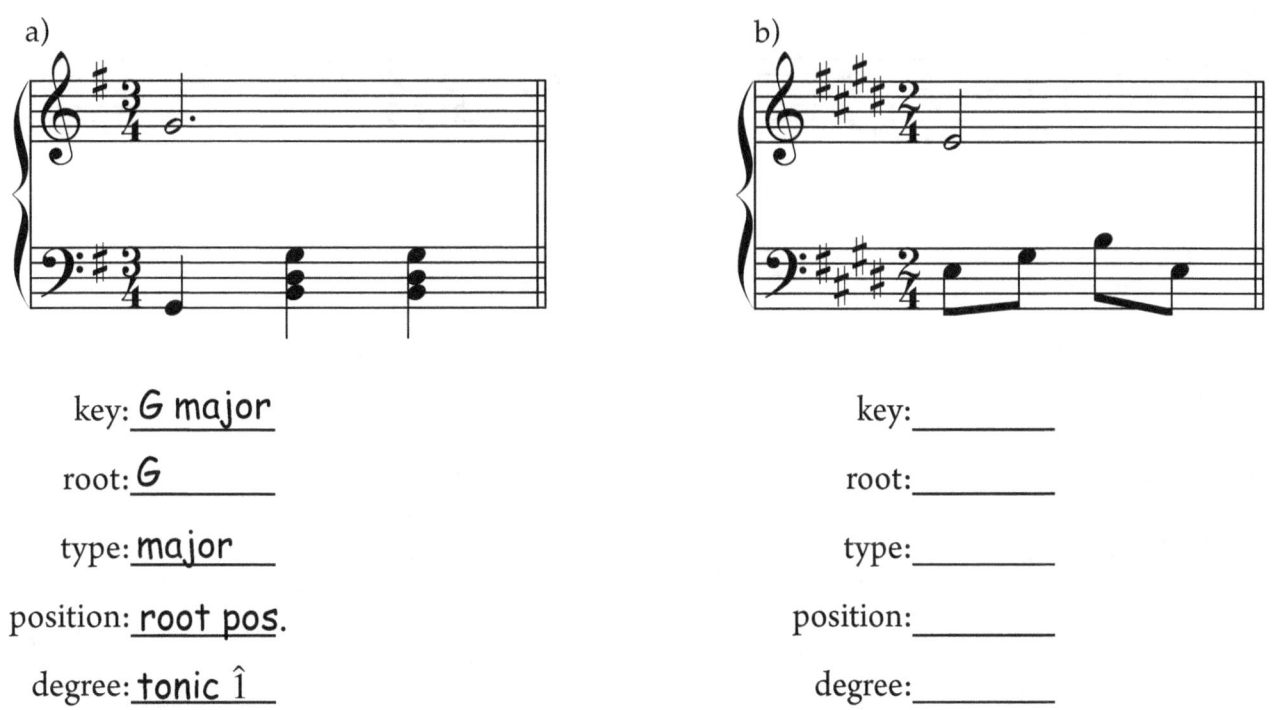

1. Name the major key of the following musical fragments. State the root, type, position, and scale degree of the triads found in each.

a)

key: G major

root: G

type: major

position: root pos.

degree: tonic $\hat{1}$

b)

key: ________

root: ________

type: ________

position: ________

degree: ________

c)

key:_____

root:_____

type:_____

position:_____

degree:_____

d)

key:_____

root:_____

type:_____

position:_____

degree:_____

e)

key:_____

root:_____

type:_____

position:_____

degree:_____

f)

key:_____

root:_____

type:_____

position:_____

degree:_____

2. Name the minor key of the following musical fragments. State the root, type, position, and scale degree of the triads found in each.

a)

key:_____

root:_____

type:_____

position:_____

degree:_____

b)

key:_____

root:_____

type:_____

position:_____

degree:_____

c)

key:_____

root:_____

type:_____

position:_____

degree:_____

d)

key:_____

root:_____

type:_____

position:_____

degree:_____

e)

key:_____
root:_____
type:_____
position:_____
degree:_____

f)

key:_____
root:_____
type:_____
position:_____
degree:_____

g)

key:_____
root:_____
type:_____
position:_____
degree:_____

h)

key:_____
root:_____
type:_____
position:_____
degree:_____

Cadences

A **cadence** is a place of rest in music. Cadences are two chord progressions that occur at the ends of phrases and at the end of a piece of music. There are two types of cadences: *final* and *non-final*.

The Authentic Cadence

The **authentic cadence** is the most common cadence. It consists of the dominant triad moving to the tonic triad (V - I). Since it ends on the tonic, it is considered to be a final cadence.

Cadences in keyboard style are written with the root of each chord in the bass clef, and the root, third, and fifth of each chord in the treble clef in close position. Authentic cadences in minor keys are much the same as those in major keys except in a minor key, the leading tone in the dominant chord must be raised.

An authentic cadence most often occurs over two measures, with the dominant chord on the last (or second last) beat of the first measure and the tonic chord on the first beat of the second measure.

Study the following authentic cadences.

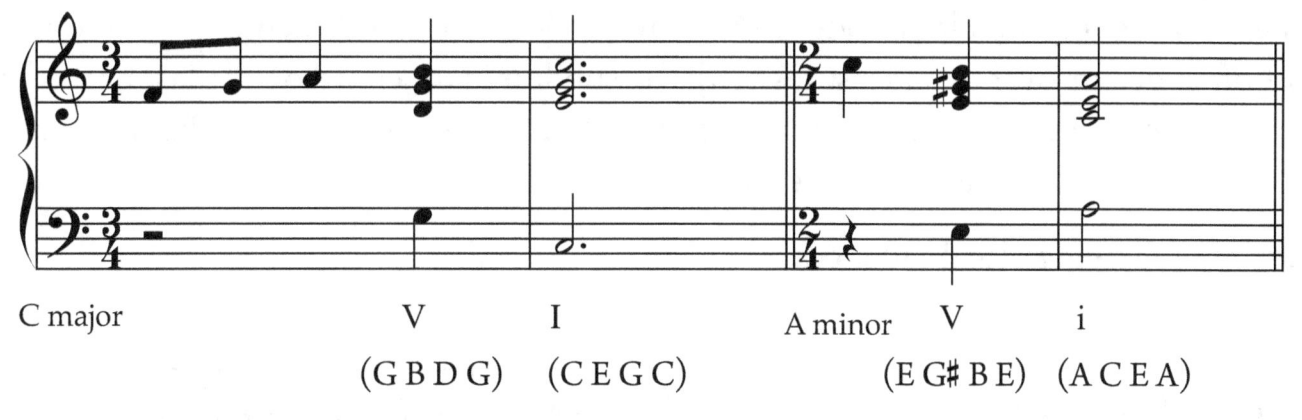

C major   V   I   A minor   V   i
            (G B D G) (C E G C)   (E G♯ B E) (A C E A)

V^7 - I

The progression V^7 - I is also an authentic cadence. In this progression, the dominant 7th can be written as a complete chord with the root in the bass and the third, fifth, and seventh in the treble. It may also be written as an incomplete chord, leaving out the fifth with the root in the bass and a doubled root, third, and seventh in the treble. In some four part writing, the seventh of V^7 must fall to the third of the I chord. In keyboard and instrumental style, this is not necessary.

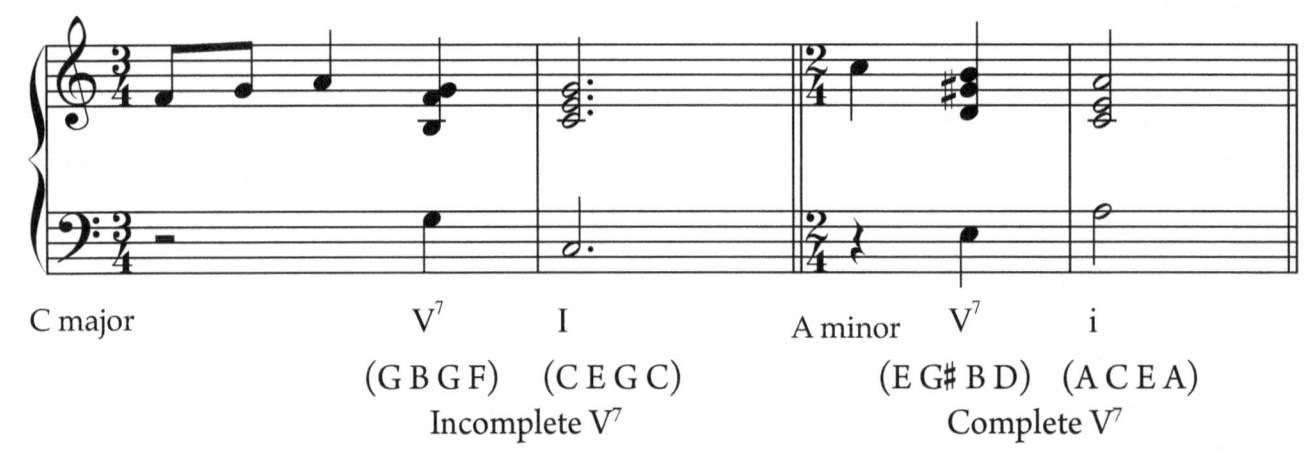

C major V^7 I   A minor V^7 i

(G B G F)   (C E G C)   (E G♯ B D)   (A C E A)

Incomplete V^7 Complete V^7

The Plagal Cadence

In a **plagal cadence**, the subdominant chord moves to the tonic chord (IV - I). Like the authentic cadence, the plagal cadence is a final cadence because it ends on the tonic. It most often occurs over two measures, with the subdominant chord on the last beat of the first measure, and the tonic chord on the first beat of the second measure. Plagal cadences often harmonize the "Amen" at the end of hymn.

Study the following plagal cadences.

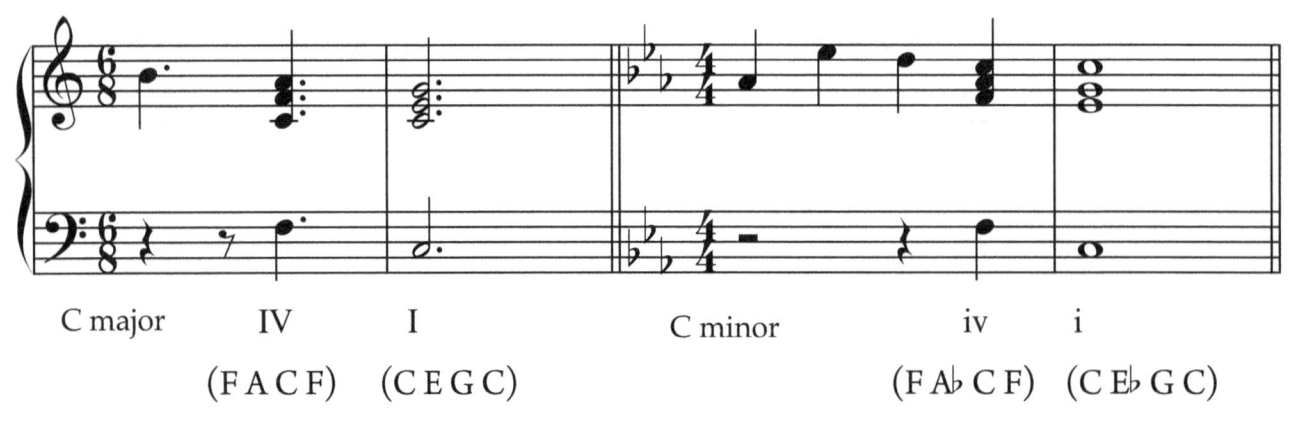

C major   IV   I   C minor   iv   i

(F A C F)   (C E G C)   (F A♭ C F)   (C E♭ G C)

1. For each of the following, name the key, name the cadence (authentic or plagal), and symbolize the chords (V - I or IV - I).

key:_____ ___ ___

cadence: _____

key:_____ ___ ___

cadence: _____

key:_____ ___ ___

cadence: _____

key:_____ ___ ___

cadence: _____

key:_____ ___ ___

cadence: _____

key:_____ ___ ___

cadence: _____

key:_____ ___ ___

cadence: _____

key:_____ ___ ___

cadence: _____

The Half Cadence

So far we have studied two types of cadences: the authentic cadence (V - I or V⁷ - I) and the plagal cadence (IV - I). Because these cadences end on the tonic chord, they give a sense of completeness or finality, like the period of a sentence. They are often used at the end of a piece of music.

The **half cadence** has an unfinished sound, like a comma, rather than a period. The imperfect cadence is also known as a **half close**. The second chord of a half cadence is always the dominant (V) chord. The first chord maybe one of many. The chords that we will use before the dominant in this lesson are the tonic (I) and the subdominant (IV). Therefore, the two half cadences that we will study our I - V and IV - V. In a half cadence, the first chord (I or IV) is usually on a weaker beat, and the dominant chord is on a stronger beat.

Study the half cadences below.

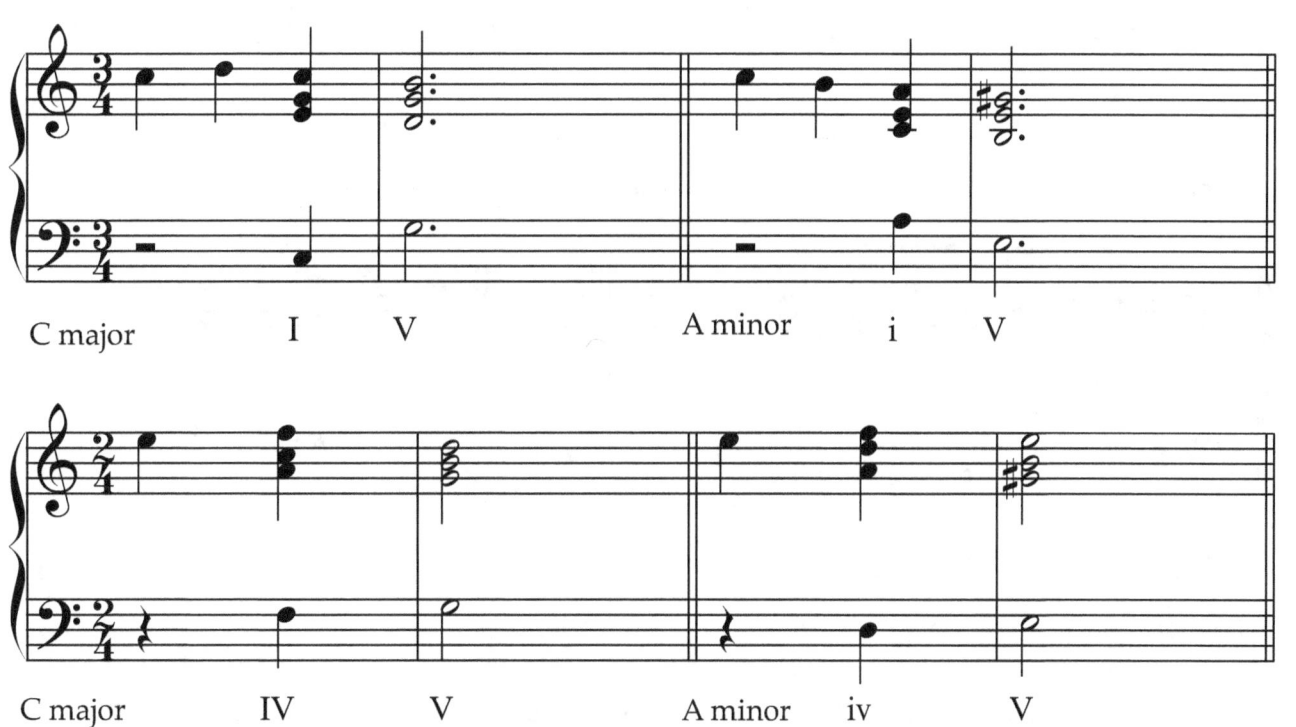

Half cadences in the minor key contain the raised leading tone in the V chord.

1. For each of the following, name the key, name the cadence (authentic or plagal, or half), and symbolize the chords.

key:_____ ___ ___

cadence:_____

key:_____ ___ ___

cadence:_____

key:_____ ___ ___

cadence:_____

key:_____ ___ ___

cadence:_____

key:_____ ___ ___

cadence:_____

key:_____ ___ ___

cadence:_____

key:_____ ___ ___

cadence:_____

key:_____ ___ ___

cadence:_____

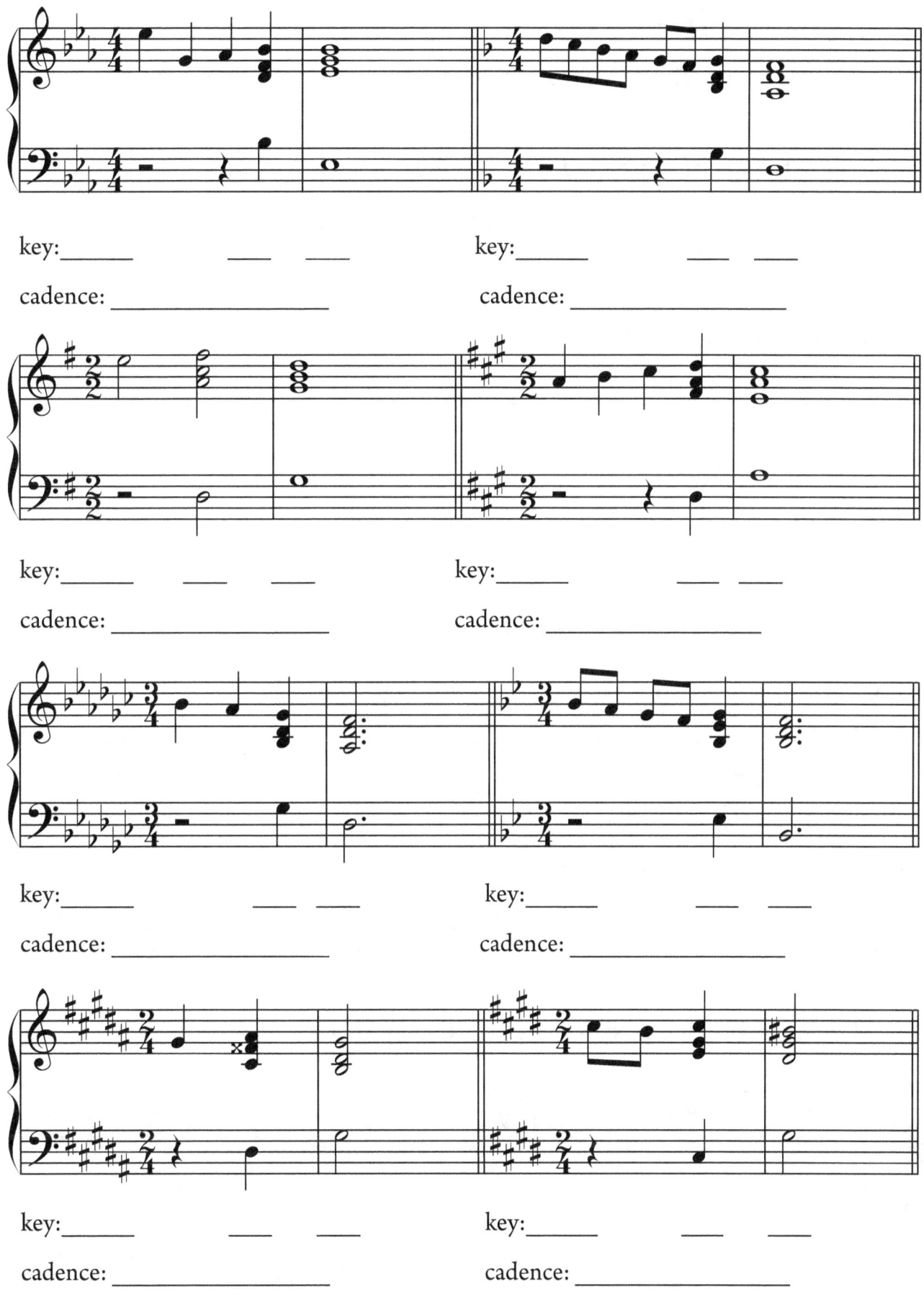

Review Three

100

1. Write the following scales ascending and descending, using the correct key signature for each.

G♭ major in the treble clef, from mediant to mediant

25

A♭ melodic minor in the bass clef, from dominant to dominant

G♯ harmonic minor in the treble clef, from tonic to tonic

D♭ major in the bass clef, from leading tone to leading tone

F♯ major in the treble clef, from supertonic to supertonic

2. Name the root, type, and position of the following triads.

15

root: _____   _____   _____   _____   _____

type: _____   _____   _____   _____   _____

position: _____   _____   _____   _____   _____

3. Write the following triads using accidentals instead of a key signature.

20

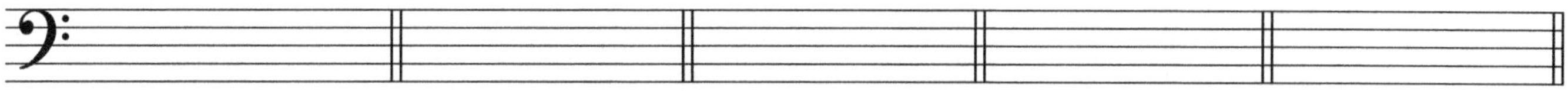

| B minor in 1st inversion | E♭ major in root position | C♯ minor in 2nd inversion | A major in 1st inversion | F♯ minor in root position |

4. For each of the following cadences, name the key, write the Roman numerals, and identify the cadences as authentic, plagal or half.

18

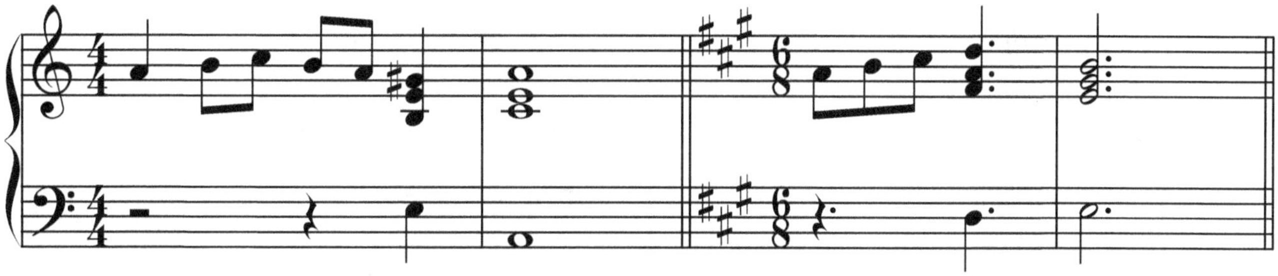

key:_____ ___ ___   key:_____ ___ ___

cadence: _____   cadence: _____

key:_____ ___ ___   key:_____ ___ ___

cadence: _____   cadence: _____

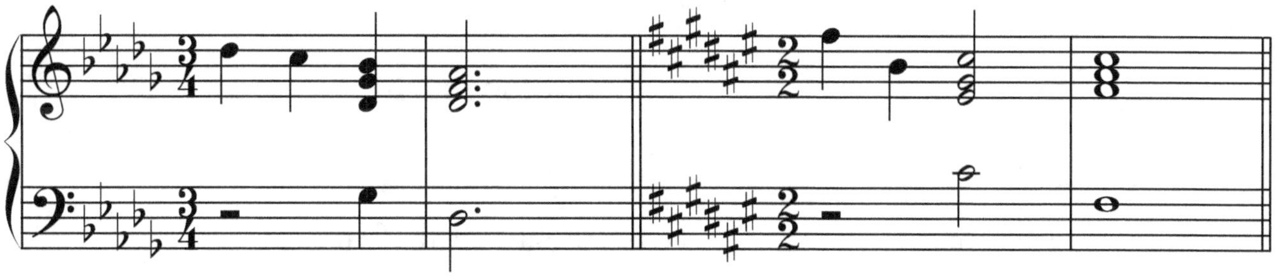

key:_____ ___ ___   key:_____ ___ ___

cadence: _____   cadence: _____

96

5. Match the following Italian terms with their definitions. (This question may contain terms from the Basic level list).

22

_____ sempre   (a) with movement

_____ piu mosso   (b) well

_____ poco   (c) much, very much

_____ senza   (d) one string, depress the left (piano) pedal

_____ vivace   (e) alway, continuosly

_____ troppo   (f) lively, brisk

_____ quasi   (g) in the manner of

_____ tenuto   (h) light, nimble, quick

_____ tempo   (i) little by little

_____ poco a poco   (j) held, sustained

_____ rubato   (k) little

_____ ottava, 8va   (l) a flexible tempo, using slight variations of speed to enhance musical expression

_____ Tempo primo   (m) more movement, quicker

_____ non troppo   (n) return to the original tempo

_____ una corda   (o) more

_____ non   (p) speed at which music is performed

_____ piu   (q) quiet, tranquil

_____ assai   (r) without

_____ ben   (s) not too much

_____ con moto   (t) not

_____ leggiero   (u) the interval of an octave

_____ tranquillo   (v) too much

Transposition

Transposition involves writing or playing music at a different pitch or in a different key. Here we will learn to transpose a melody from one major key to another major key.

To transpose a melody into a new key, you must know the original key of the melody and either the new key or the interval of transposition. If the interval of transposition is given, you must determine the new key.

Here is a melody in G major.

To transpose this melody up a major 3rd, follow these four steps.

1. Determine the original key. The original key is G major.
2. Find the note that is a major 3rd above G. This note will be the tonic of the new key. A major third above G is B. The new key will B major.
3. Write the key signature of the new key. B major has a key signature of five sharps.
4. Move each note of the original melody up a 3rd. (Note that because we have used the key signature of the new key, every one of these thirds will be a major third.)

Here is the melody transposed into B Major.

If a melody contains accidentals, the transposed melody will also contain accidentals. If a note in the original melody is raised, the corresponding transposed note must be raised. If a note in the original melody is lowered, the corresponding transposed note must be lowered.

In the following example, the original melody in B flat major has been transposed up a major 2nd to C major. The original melody contains two accidentals: E natural (m. 2) and B natural (m. 3). Both of these notes have been raised one half step.

This means that the corresponding notes in the transposed melody (F and C) must also be raised one half step: F sharp (m. 2) and C sharp (m. 3).

1. Name the key of the following melody.

(a) Transpose it up a perfect 4th and name the new key.
(b) Transpose it up a minor 3rd and name the new key.

Traditional African

key:_____

key:_____

key:_____

2. Name the key of the following melody.

(a) Transpose it up a major 2nd and name the new key.
(b) Transpose it into the key of F♯ major.

key:_____

key:_____

3. Name the key of the following melody.

(a) Transpose it into the key of B major
(b) Transpose it up a major 3rd and name the new key.

key:_____

key:_____

4. Name the key of the following melody.

(a) Transpose it up a perfect 5th and name the new key.
(b) Transpose it up a major 2nd and name the new key.

George Frideric Handel

key:_____

key:_____

key:_____

5. Name the key of the following melody.

(a) Transpose it into the key of D♭ major
(b) Transpose it up a minor 6th and name the new key.

Franz Schubert

key:_____

key:_____

6. Name the key of the following melody.

(a) Transpose it up a perfect 4th and name the new key.
(b) Transpose it into the key of A major.

key:_____

key:_____

7. Learn the following Italian terms and their definitions.

e, ed	and
fortepiano **fp**	loud then suddenly soft
grave	slow and solemn
loco	return to the normal register
ma	but
meno	less
meno mosso	less movement, slower
M.M.	metronome marking (Maelzel's Metronome)
molto	much, very

Review Four

1. Name the keys of the following melodies. Rewrite them using key signatures.

key:_____

key:_____

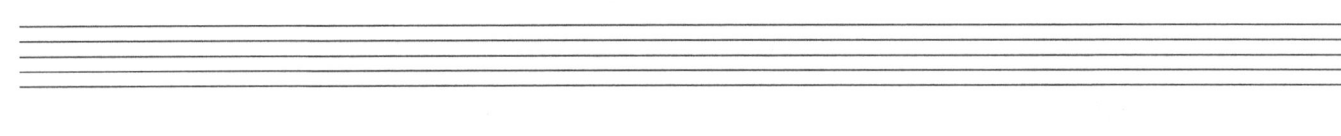

key:_____

2. Name the key of the following melody.

    (a) Transpose it up a major 3rd and name the new key.
    (b) Transpose it up a perfect 4th and name the new key.
    (c) Transpose it up a perfect 5th and name the new key.
    (d) Transpose it into the key of A major.

40

Edvard Grieg

key:_____

key:_____

key:_____

key:_____

3. Match the following Italian terms with their definitions.

____ molto (a) without
____ grave (b) almost, as if
____ fortepiano (c) much, very
____ e, ed (d) metronome marking
____ loco (e) less movement, slower
____ ma (f) lively, brisk
____ meno (g) held, sustained
____ M.M. (h) expressive, with expresssion
____ meno mosso (i) return to normal register
____ vivace (j) and
____ tenuto (k) less
____ quasi (l) slow and solemn
____ ben (m) but
____ espressivo (n) well
____ senza (o) loud then suddenly soft

Musical Analysis

1. Analyze the following music by answering the questions below.

(a) Define *allegretto* _____

(b) Name the composer of this excerpt: _____

(c) Add the time signature to the music.

(d) For the chord at A, name the root:_____ type:_____ position:_____

(e) Name the intervals at B: _____ C:_____

(f) Explain the sign at D: _____

(g) Explain the sign at E: _____

(h) Name the key of this excerpt: _____

(i) How many measures are in this excerpt?_____

2. Analyze the following music by answering the questions below.

Sonatina
Anh.5/1

Ludwig van Beethoven
(1770-1827)

Moderato

(a) Name the key of this excerpt._____

(b) Name the composer of this excerpt:_____

(c) Add the time signature to the music.

(d) Define *moderato*:_____

(e) Name the intervals at A: _____ B:_____

(f) Explain the sign at C: _____

(g) Classify the chords at:
　　D: root: _____ type: _____ position:_____
　　E: root: _____ type: _____ position:_____

(h) How many measures are in this excerpt?_____

3. Analyze the following music by answering the questions below.

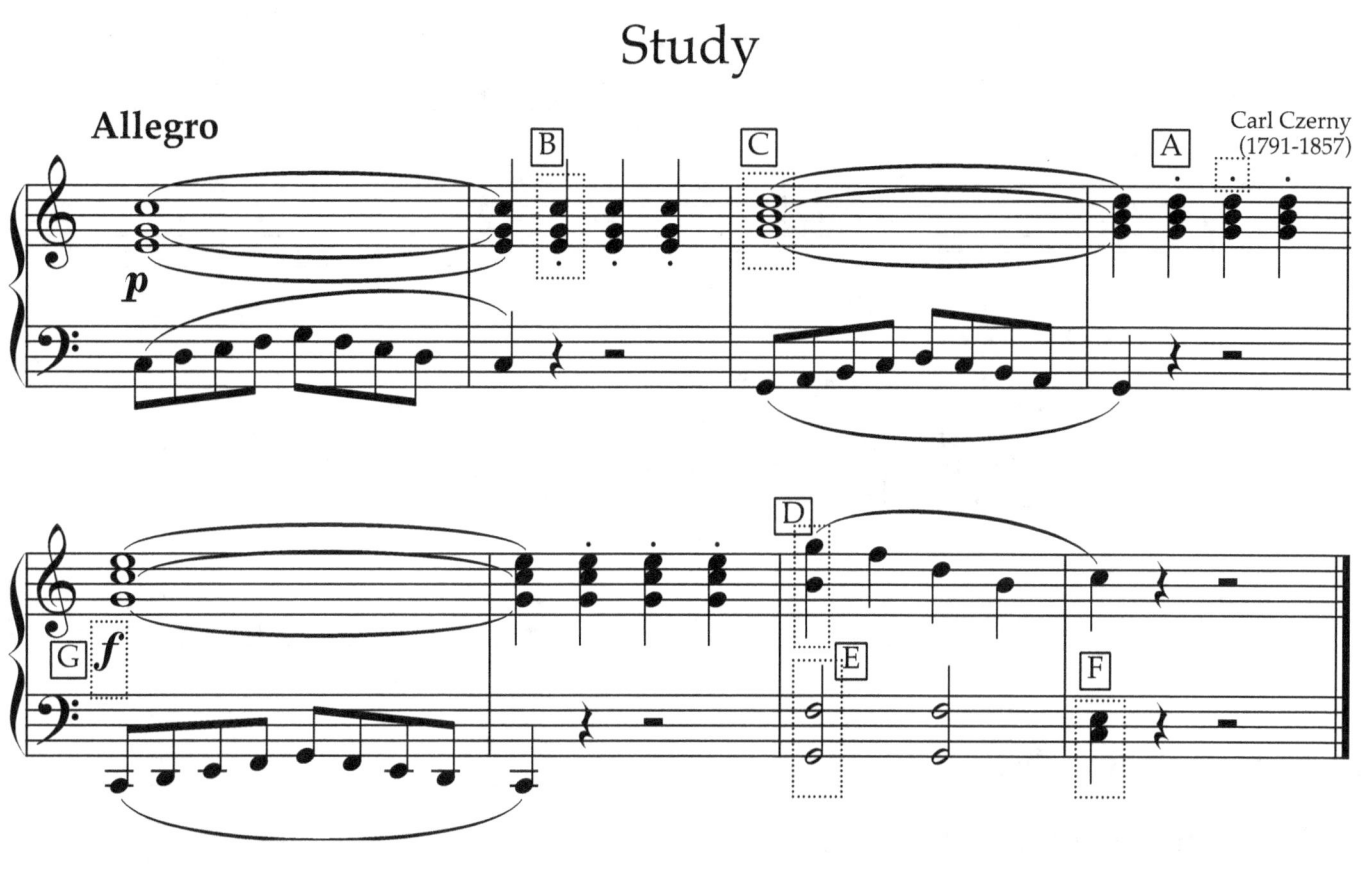

(a) Name the key of this excerpt._____

(b) Name the composer of this excerpt:_____

(c) Add the time signature to the music.

(d) Define *allegro*:_____

(e) Explain the sign at A: _____

(f) Classify the chords at:
   B: root: _____ type: _____ position: _____
   C: root: _____ type: _____ position: _____

(g) How many measures are in this excerpt?_____

(h) Name the intervals at D: _____ E: _____ F: _____

(i) Explain the sign at G: _____

4. Analyze the following music by answering the questions below.

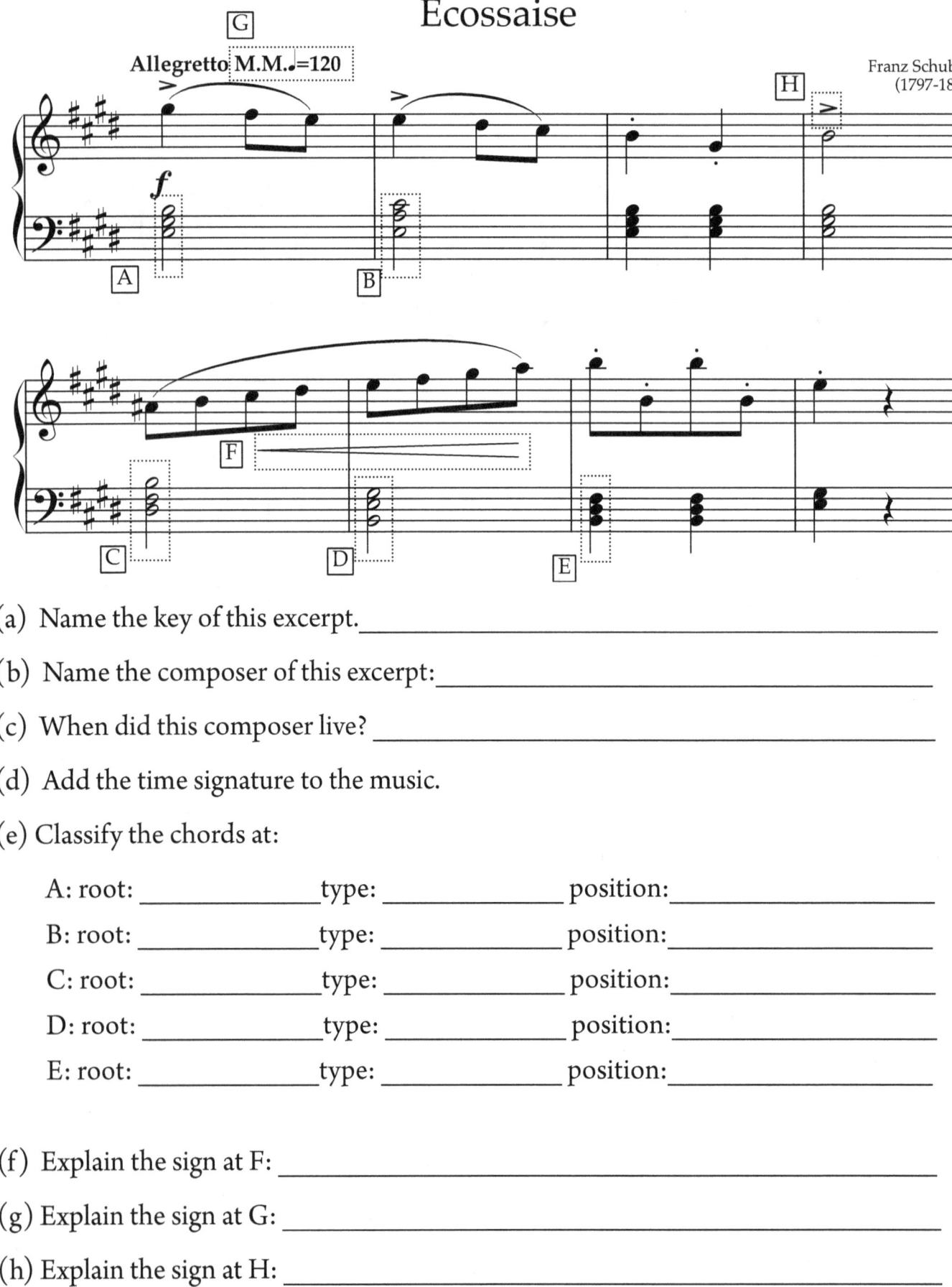

(a) Name the key of this excerpt. _____

(b) Name the composer of this excerpt: _____

(c) When did this composer live? _____

(d) Add the time signature to the music.

(e) Classify the chords at:

  A: root: _____ type: _____ position: _____

  B: root: _____ type: _____ position: _____

  C: root: _____ type: _____ position: _____

  D: root: _____ type: _____ position: _____

  E: root: _____ type: _____ position: _____

(f) Explain the sign at F: _____

(g) Explain the sign at G: _____

(h) Explain the sign at H: _____

Practice Test

1. Name the following intervals.

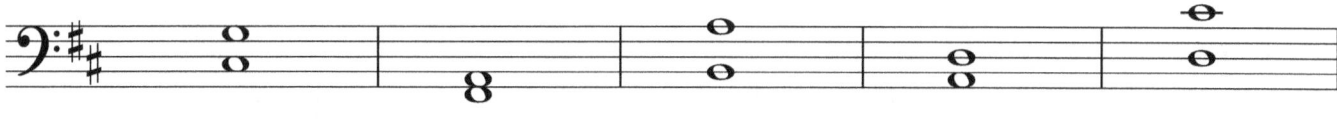

_____   _____   _____   _____   _____

2. Invert the above intervals and rename them.

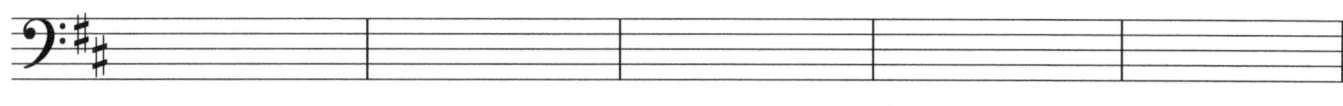

_____   _____   _____   _____   _____

3. Write the following triads, using a key signature for each.
   (a) the tonic triad of B♭ major
   (b) the dominant triad of C♯ minor
   (c) the subdominant triad of D♭ major
   (d) the supertonic triad of F♯ major
   (e) the mediant triad of A♭ minor

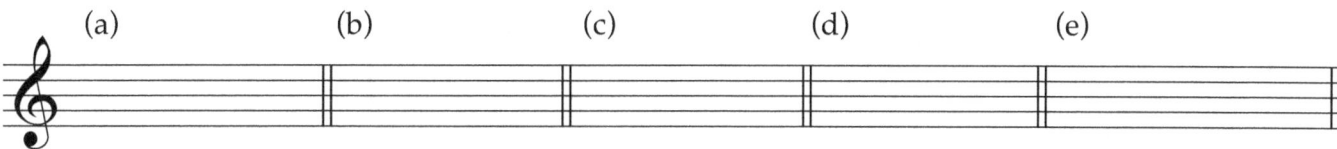

4. Name each of the following scales as major, natural minor, harmonic minor, melodic minor, whole tone, major pentatonic, minor pentatonic, blues, chromatic, or octatonic.

_____

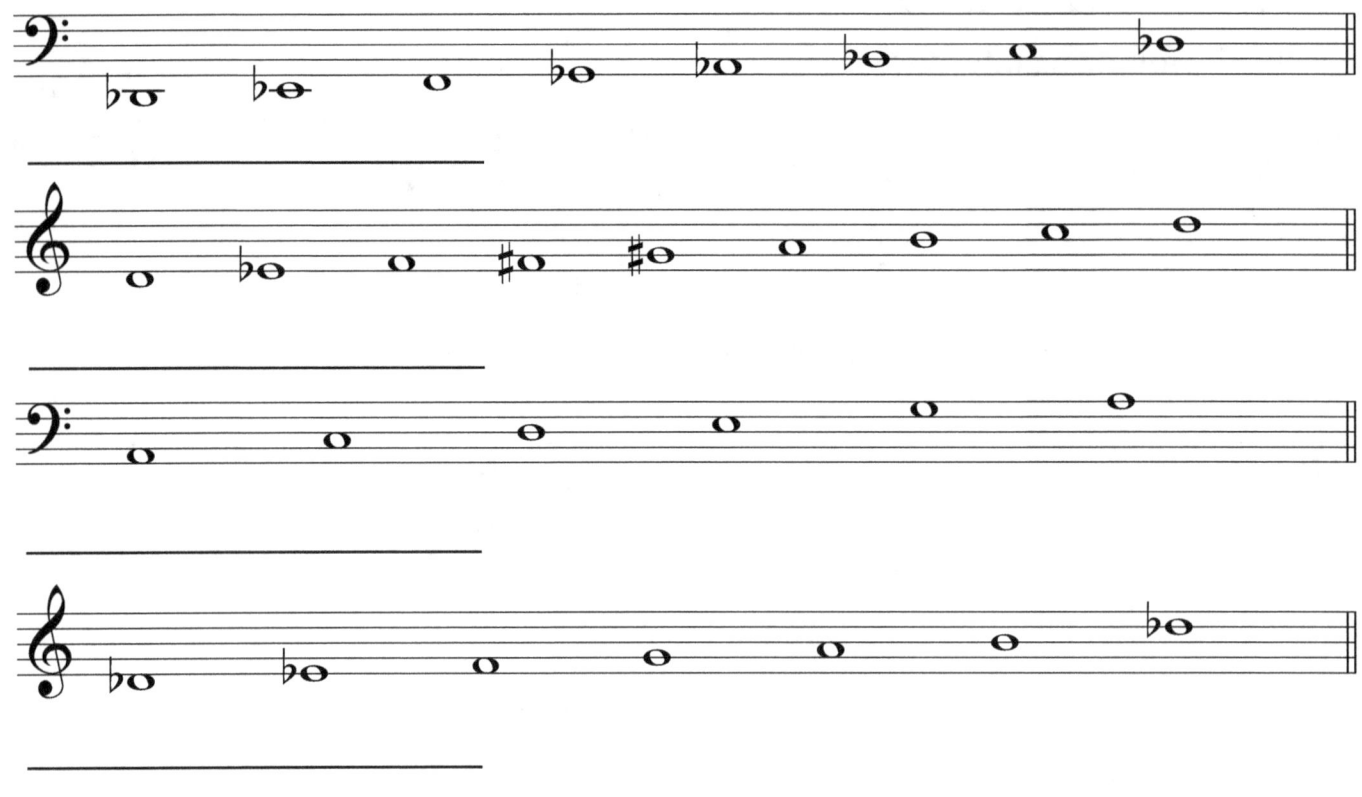

10

5 Name the key of the following melody. Transpose it up a minor 6th, and name the new key.

key:_____

key:_____

6. Add rests under the brackets to complete the following one measure rhythms.
10

7. Add time signatures to the following one measure rhythms.
10

10

8. Name the key of the following musical fragments. Write the chord symbols at the end of each and name the cadence as authentic, plagal, or half.

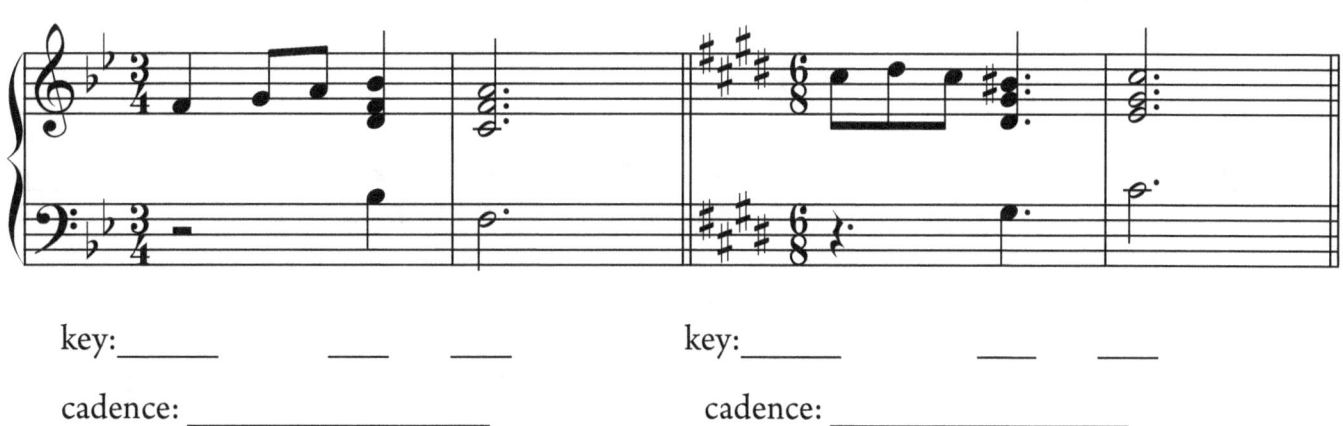

key:_____   ___ ___   key:_____   ___ ___

cadence: _____   cadence: _____

9. (a) Name the minor key of each key signature.
   (b) Name the degree of the scale for each note.

   _____
   10

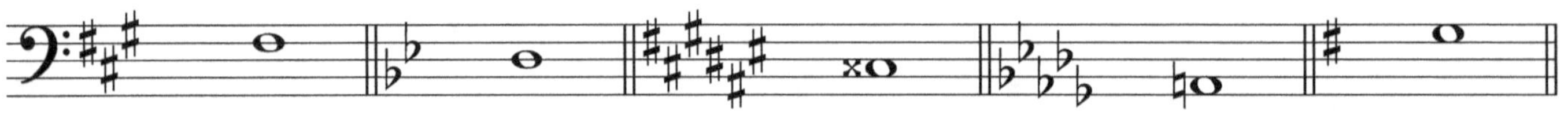

   (a) _____   _____   _____   _____   _____
   (b) _____   _____   _____   _____   _____

   _____
   10

10. Rewrite the following melodies, omitting the accidentals and using key signatures. Name the key of each melody.

   key:_____

   key:_____

11. Analyze the following piece of music by answering the questions below.

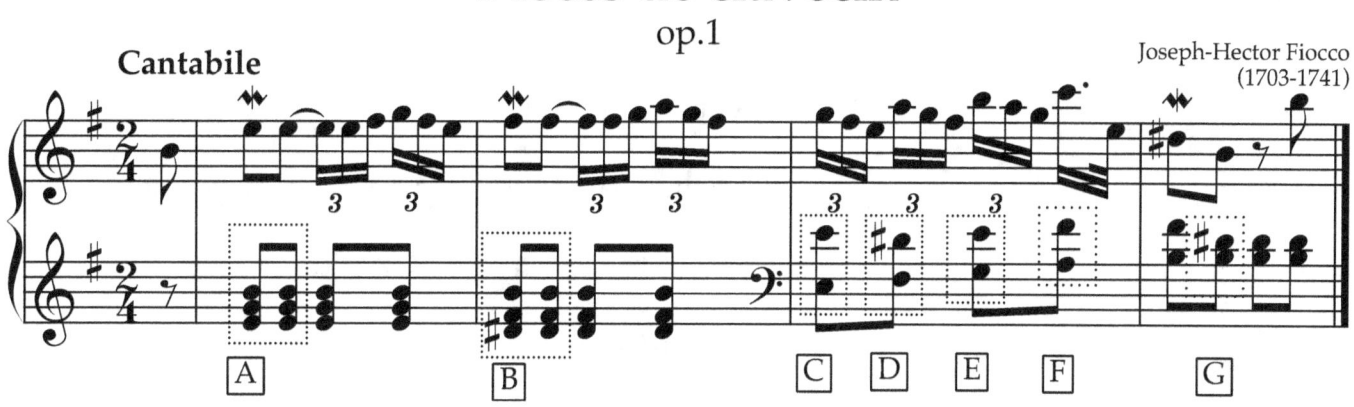

(a) Name the key of this excerpt. _____

(b) Name the composer of this excerpt: _____

(c) Add the time signature to the music.

(d) Classify the chords at:

    A: root: _____ type: _____ position: _____

    B: root: _____ type: _____ position: _____

(e) Name the intervals at C: _____ D: _____

    E: _____ F: _____ G: _____

(f) Define cantabile: _____

GRADE

Terms and Signs

accelerando, accel.	becoming quicker
alla, all'	in the manner of
animato	lively, animated
assai	much, very much (*allegro assai*: very fast)
ben, bene	well (*ben marcato*: well marked)
brillante	brilliant
col ,coll', colla, colle	with (*coll'ottava*: with an added octave)
con	with
con brio	with vigor or spirit
con espressione.	with expression
con moto	with movement
e, ed	and
espressivo, espress.	expressive, with expression
fortepiano, **fp**	loud then suddenly soft
grave	slow and solemn
leggiero	light, numble, quick
ma	but
meno	less
meno mosso	less movement, slower
M.M.	metronome marking
molto	much, very
non	not
non troppo	not too much

piu	more
piu mosso	more movement, quicker
poco	little
poco a poco	little by little
quasi	almost, as if
rubato	a flexible tempo using slight variations of speed to enhance musical expression
sempre	always
senza	without
spiritoso	spirited
tenuto	held, sustained
tranquillo	tranquil
tre corde	three strings, release the left piano pedal
troppo	too much
una corda	one string, press the left piano pedal
vivace	lively brisk

History

George Frideric Handel (1685 - 1759) Baroque Era

George Frideric Handel was born on February 23, 1685, in Halle Germany. His father, a barber-surgeon, wanted his son to be a lawyer. However, Handel loved music and practiced on a small keyboard instrument called a clavichord, given to him by his aunt.

In 1693, while visiting the royal court, Handel had an opportunity to play the great organ. When the Duke heard him play, he convinced his father to give him musical training. Handel studied with the organist of St. Michel's in Halle. He learned how to compose, and how to play violin and oboe as well as organ and harpsichord.

In 1702, Handel followed his father's suggestion and entered law school at the University of Halle. After his father's death in the following year, he left his law studies and accepted a position as the organist at Halle Cathedral. The following year, he moved to Hamburg and worked as a violinist and harpsichordist at the opera house. It was there that Handel's first operas were written and produced.

In 1710, Handel accepted the position of Kapellmeister to George, Elector of Hanover, who was soon to be King George I of Great Britain. In 1712, he settled in England where George's wife Queen Anne gave him a yearly income.

Handel wrote operas and oratorios plus music for instruments and ensembles. In 1727, he applied for British citizenship and adopted England as his new home. When King George I died, Handel wrote the music for the coronation of the new king. *Zadok the Priest*, one of these compositions, is still performed today at British coronations.

By 1741, Handel had completed the oratorio Messiah. The first performance of Messiah was given in Ireland in 1742 and was a great success. Many people, to this day, stand during the performance of the "Hallelujah Chorus." Some historians disagree, but the legend is that when the king first heard the "Hallelujah Chorus" he rose to his feet, overcome with emotion. Since the king stood, so did the entire audience. The tradition continues to this day of standing when the "Hallelujah Chorus" from Messiah is performed.

Handel died on April 14, 1759. He was given the honor of a state funeral and was buried in Westminster Abby in London, England. More than 3,000 people attended his funeral.

What is an Oratorio?

An *oratorio* is a large composition for orchestra, choir, and soloists based on a religious theme. Some of the components of an oratorio are:

- *overture* - the musical introduction to the oratorio.
- *recitative* - a kind of musical declamation used during the oratorio, sung in the rhythm of ordinary speech often with many words on the same note.
- *aria* - an accompanied song for a solo voice.
- *chorus* - a large group of singers that performs together with an orchestra.

Messiah

Messiah is an oratorio composed in 1741 by George Frideric Handel. The ***libretto,*** which is the term used for the text of the oratorio, is based on verses from the Old and New Testaments of the Bible.

It is believed that Handel composed Messiah in only three or four weeks in August and September of 1741. What makes this amazing is the scale of this work. The score is 259 pages, and it takes nearly two hours to perform.

The "Hallelujah Chorus" from Messiah

The "Hallelujah Chorus" is part of Handel's Messiah. It is written for a chorus consisting of soprano, alto, tenor and bass with orchestra. The voices in a four part chorus are:

- *soprano* - sung by womens high voices
- *alto* - sung by womens low voices
- *tenor* - sung by mens high voices
- *bass* - sung by mens low voices

The text for "Hallelujah Chorus" comes from the book of Revelation in the New Testament. The word 'Hallelujah' means praise the Lord and is used in worship as an expression of rejoicing.
Text:
>Hallelujah!
>For the Lord God omnipotent reigneth;
>The kingdom of this world is become the kingdom of our Lord and of his Christ;
>and He shall reign for ever and ever.
>King of Kings and Lord of Lords.
>Hallelujah!

The example below is the opening of the chorus from the Hallelujah Chorus. Each voice part of the chorus receives its own staff line.

Hallelujah Chorus uses a technique called **word painting**. Word painting, sometimes called tone painting or text painting, is the technique of writing music that mirrors the actual meaning of a song.

In Hallelujah chorus low notes symbolize the world while the kingdom of the Lord is sung on high notes. The Hallelujah section has a joyful sound characterized by arpeggios and chromatic notes occurring in a major scale. The line *"for ever and ever"* is repeated over and over.

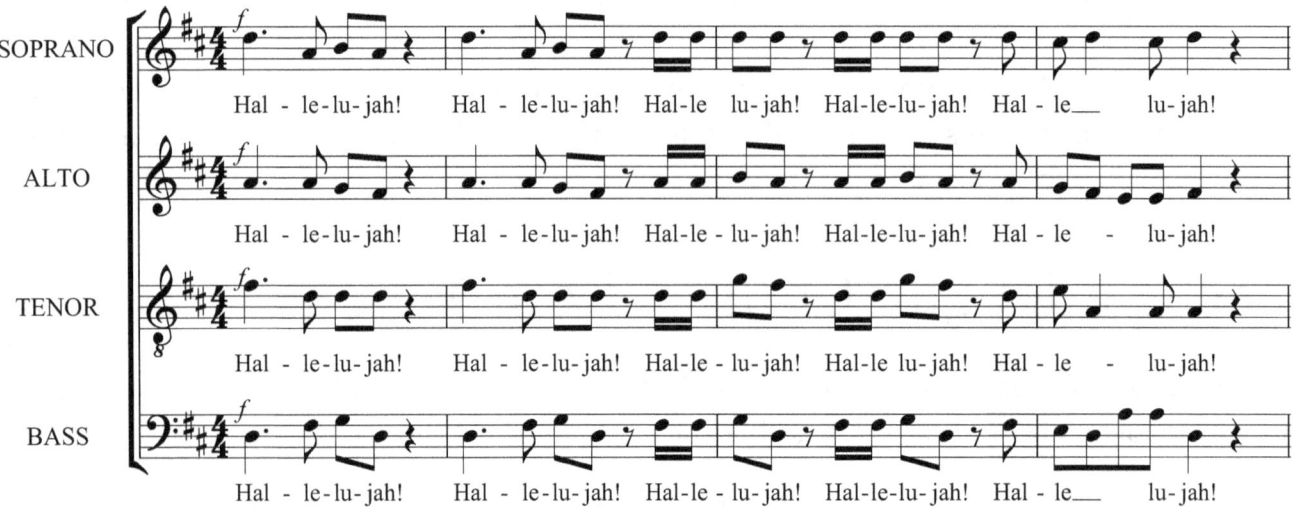

Wolfgang Amadeus Mozart (1756 - 1791) Classical Era

Wolfgang Amadeus Mozart was born in Salzburg, Austria, on January 27, 1756. He was born into a family of musicians and was an incredible child prodigy. Under the strong influence of his father, Mozart began composing music at the age of five! Here is a brief timeline of his life:

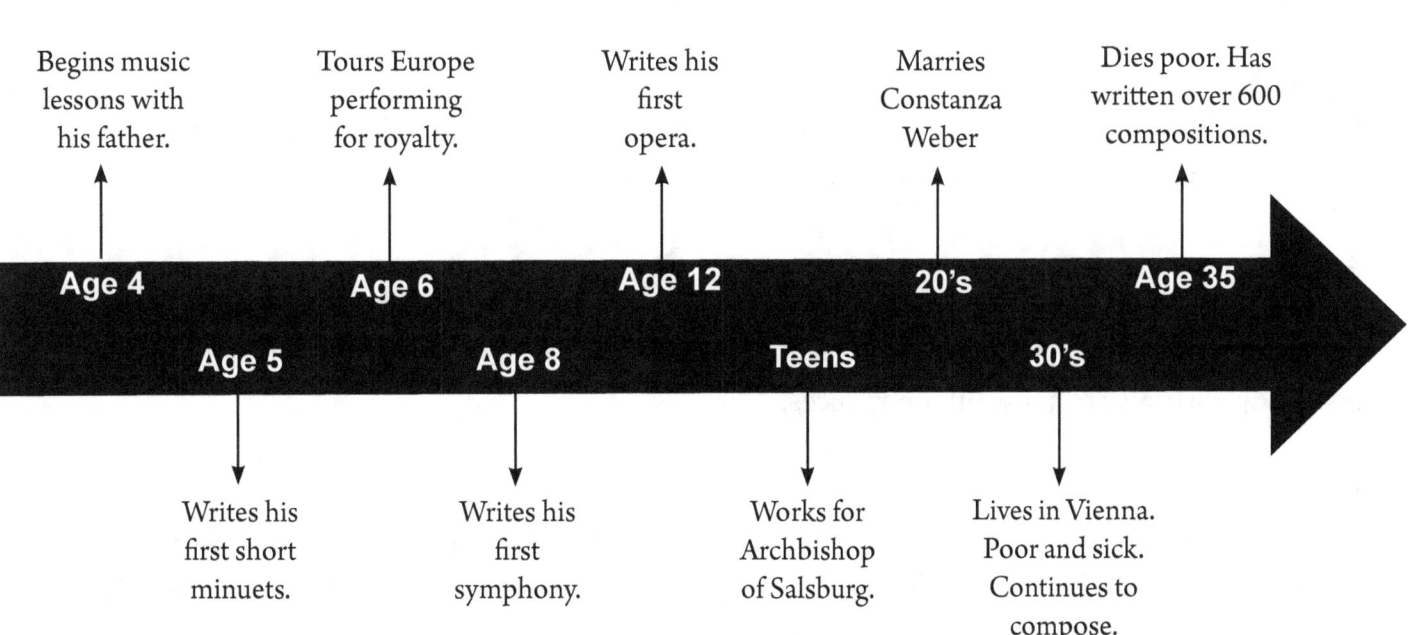

Opera

An *opera* is a play with music. The actual word "opera" is Italian for "work" and was first used in England in 1656. The earliest Italian operas were called favola in musica (fable in music) and drama per musica (drama by means of music).

The construction of an opera is like that of a play. It can be anywhere from one to five acts, and last anywhere from 30 minutes to five hours. The average opera is usually about 3 hours long. Like plays, operas are staged and use sets and costumes.

Operas usually begin with an **overture**. An overture is a piece of music played by the orchestra that contains melodies from the main part of the opera. The purpose of the overture is to inform the audience that the opera is starting and to set the mood.

Elements of an Opera

Here are some of the elements that are found in an opera:

Recitatives
Recitatives are simple melodies sung at the speed of normal speech. There were originally accompanied by a harpsichord, and in later operas, by the orchestra.

Arias
Arias are songs that can be taken out of an opera and sung as separate musical performances. Most operas are remembered for their finest arias. Arias are often challenging to perform, and give singers the opportunity to show off their voices.

Ensembles
Ensembles occur when characters in the opera sing together. They range from short duets to long, complex pieces involving many characters. Some of Mozart's ensembles can last for 20 minutes!

Choruses
A chorus is a group of singers, singing together. They supply the crowd scenes and extra characters in the opera, as well as the opportunity for beautiful choral music. Members of the chorus may portray servants, party guests, or other unnamed characters.

The Magic Flute (1791)

Mozart's famous opera, **The Magic Flute, Die Zauberflöte** in German, was composed in 1791. The **libretto** or text of the opera was written by Emanuel Schikaneder. It tells a fanciful and extraordinary story that includes a bird seller, a princess, a young prince who wants to rescue her, an evil Queen of the Night, a wise priest, and of course, a magic flute. The story is very complicated, but the music is beautiful and unforgettable.

The Magic Flute is a genre or type of opera called **Singspiel**. Singspiel (pronounced "zing-shpeel") originated in German-speaking countries and found its roots in comic opera. The translation of singspiel is "sing-play." It includes spoken dialogue between the singing, and often, an exotic or fanciful theme.

The Magic Flute is the most famous example of Singspiel. When Mozart was composing, opera was dominated by Italian traditions and language. Mozart decided to write this opera in German as a way to show pride and love of his country and culture and to connect with the common people, not just the elite. It contains a diverse cast of characters and some of Mozart's most magnificent music.

Queen of the Night Aria from "The Magic Flute"

"Der Hölle Rache kocht in meinem Herzen" ("Hell's vengeance boils in my heart"), is an aria sung by the Queen of the Night, in the second act of The Magic Flute. It is often called "The Queen of the Night Aria." In it, the Queen of the Night, who is in a tremendous rage, places a knife into the hand of her daughter Pamina and demands that she assassinate Sarastro, the Queen's rival.

The Queen of the Night is sung by a *coloratura soprano*. Sopranos sing in the highest range of the four voice parts. However, coloratura sopranos are capable of seemingly superhuman feats. In the Queen of the Night aria, the voice is extremely agile, firing out fast paced notes that ascend as high as the 3rd F above middle C. Coloratura soprano roles have existed from Baroque through 20th century opera.

An amazing performance of this aria by the gifted soprano Diana Damrau can be found on YouTube.

The example below is the opening measures of Der Hölle Rache kocht in meinem Herzen. The piano part is the orchestral reduction. The key is in D minor. **Allegro assai** means very fast.

The excerpt below shows the incredible virtuosity employed by the coloratura soprano in this aria.

This is the text for Der Hölle Rache kocht in meinem Herzen in German with English translation.

Der Hölle Rache kocht in meinem Herzen,	The vengeance of Hell boils in my heart,
Tod und Verzweiflung flammet um mich her!	Death and despair flame about me!
Fühlt nicht durch dich Sarastro	If Sarastro does not through you feel
Todesschmerzen,	The pain of death,
So bist du meine Tochter nimmermehr.	Then you will be my daughter nevermore.
Verstossen sei auf ewig,	Disowned may you be forever,
Verlassen sei auf ewig,	Abandoned may you be forever,
Zertrümmert sei'n auf ewig	Destroyed be forever
Alle Bande der Natur	All the bonds of nature,
Wenn nicht durch dich!	If not through you
Sarastro wird erblassen!	Sarastro becomes pale! (as death)
Hört, Rachegötter,	Hear, Gods of Revenge,
Hört der Mutter Schwur!	Hear a mother's oath!

Harold Arlen (1905- 1986) Modern Era

Harold Arlen was an American composer, arranger, pianist, and vocalist. He worked as a piano accompanist in vaudeville during his early twenties. His first hit song "Get Happy" was composed with Ted Koehler in 1929.

In the 1930's and 40's, Arlen wrote some of his greatest hits including the score to the movie, The Wizard of Oz. He and his co-writer won the 1939 Academy Award for Best Original Song for "Over the Rainbow."

Stormy Weather, It's Only a Paper Moon, and I've Got the World on a String, are just a few of the standards that live on today and make Harold Arlen one of the most celebrated American composers of the 20th Century.

Over the Rainbow

Harold Arlen composed "Over the Rainbow," with lyricist Edgar Yipsel Harburg, for the 1939 movie The Wizard of Oz.

In the movie, it is sung by actress and singer Judy Garland who plays the role of Dorothy Gale. This film introduced Garland's powerful voice to the public. Visit YouTube for a recording of Garland's performance. Over the Rainbow is written for solo voice and orchestra. It follows a type of song form called AABA song form. This was a standard form used during the first part of the 20th century by composers like Harold Arlen, George Gershwin, and Irving Berlin. AABA songs are usually 32 bars in length and preceded by an Introduction.

AABA song form contains an opening section (A), a bridge (B), and a final A section. It is used in a variety of music genres including pop, jazz, and gospel.
The typical AABA song form follows this outline:

(Introduction)   **A** = 8 bars   **A** = 8 bars   **B** = 8 bars   **A** = 8 bars

AABA has no separate chorus, and the title usually appears at the beginning of each A section. In Over the Rainbow, each A section begins with the lyrics "Somewhere Over the Rainbow." The B section is contrasting and brings the listener back to the last A section.

The lyrics to Over the Rainbow help to illustrate the AABA song structure form.

Introduction

When all the world is a hopeless jumble,
and the raindrops tumble all around,
heaven opens a magic lane.

When all the clouds darken up the skyway,
There's a rainbow highway to be found,
Leading from your window pane.

To a place behind the sun,
Just a step beyond the rain.

A

Somewhere over the rainbow, way up high,
There's a land that I dreamed of,
Once in a lullabye.

A

Somewhere over the rainbow, skies are blue,
And the dreams that you dare to dream,
Really do come true.

B

Someday day I'll wish upon a star,
and wake up where the clouds are far behind me.
Where troubles melt like lemon drops,
Away above the chimney tops,
That's where you'll find me.

A

Somewhere over the rainbow, skies are blue,
And the dreams that you dare to dream,
Really do come true.
If happy little bluebirds fly.
Beyond the rainbow,
Why, oh why can't I?

Answer the following questions.

a) Where was Handel born? _____

b) In what music era did Handel live? _____

c) What country did Handel adopt as his new home? _____

d) What is an oratorio? _____

e) When did Handel compose Messiah? _____

f) What voices make up the 4 parts of the chorus in Hallelujah Chorus?

_____   _____   _____   _____

g) What is word painting? _____

_____

h) Give one example of word painting in Hallelujah Chorus. _____

_____

i) What is an opera? _____

j) In what era did Mozart compose? _____

k) What year did Mozart compose "The Magic Flute?" _____

l) What genre or type of opera is "The Magic Flute?" _____

m) What language did Mozart use for "The Magic Flute?" _____

n) What is an aria? _____

_____

o) What type of soprano sings the Queen of the Night aria? _____

Choose the correct answer.

The composer of the Wizard of Oz:

☐ Harold Arlen ☐ George Gershwin ☐ Irving Berlin

Harold Arlen was:

☐ French ☐ Russian ☐ American

"Over the Rainbow" was written for:

☐ Bette Davis ☐ Judy Garland ☐ Beyonce

The song form of "Over the Rainbow" is:

☐ AABA ☐ ABBA ☐ ABAB

The Baroque Era (ca 1600 - 1750)

The word **Baroque** is used to describe a style of art from a specific period in history. *Art* can mean a lot of things. Here, it applies to painting, architecture, and most importantly to our field of study, music.

All Baroque art, architecture, and music was created around 1600 to 1750. However, Baroque music is a style of music. It is not an exact period of time.

What is the Baroque style?

Artists of the Baroque period attempted to evoke emotions in the listener by appealing to their senses. A composer could create a piece of music that would make the listener feel a specific emotion (sadness, happiness, etc.). This was known as **the doctrine of the affections**.

Baroque music is tuneful, very organized, and its melodies are often highly decorated and elaborate. This music can be quite dramatic.

A lot of Baroque music is **contrapuntal** or based on **counterpoint**. This means that there can be many different lines of music (or melodies) all going their own way. These single melodies weave together to make a whole piece of music.

The best way to understand Baroque music, is to listen to the great Baroque composers.

There are many great composers from the Baroque era. The greatest one is Johann Sebastian Bach (1685–1750).

Other famous baroque composers include:

Johann Pachelbel (1653–1706)
Antonio Vivaldi (1678–1741)
George Frideric Handel (1685–1759)

Johann Sebastian Bach (1685 - 1750)

Johann Sebastian Bach was born in Eisenach, Germany, where his father, a musician, taught him to play violin and harpsichord. By the time Johann was 10, both his parents had died. Johann was raised by his older brother who was a church organist. Johann also became a very skilled organist.

Bach's life has three major periods.

The Weimar period. Bach worked for the Duke of Weimar. In this period he became an organ virtuoso and wrote many great works for the instrument.

The Cöthen period. Bach worked for the Prince of Anhalt-Cöthen. During this period he composed a lot of chamber music including suites, instrumental sonatas, and the Brandenburg Concertos.

The Leipzig period. During this period Bach became the cantor, organist, and music composer for St. Thomas Lutheran Church in Leipzig, Germany. Bach remained there for the rest of his life.

Bach wrote music for keyboard instruments (harpsichord, clavichord, organ), orchestra, choirs, chamber groups, and many solo instruments. He is considered one of the greatest musical geniuses in history. In fact, he is such an important composer, that the year of his death (1750), is used to mark the end of the Baroque Era.

Two-part Invention in C major, BWV 772 - J.S. Bach

Bachs *Inventions and Sinfonias,* also known as the *Two and Three-Part Inventions* are a collection of thirty pieces for keyboard. There are 15 two-part and 15 three-part inventions in the masterpiece. Bach said that he composed the Inventions "for amateurs of the keyboard to achieve a cantabile style of playing in two and three parts." They were written as musical teaching pieces for his students.
The two-part inventions were composed in the Cöthen period, and the three-part inventions (Sinfonias)were completed at the beginning of the Leipzig period.

Polyphony is the performance of multiple melodies at the same time. It's a little like two people giving speeches next to each other, but the speeches are different. Imagine having four speakers giving four different speeches at the same time. Eventually, rules developed to control these multiple melodies. These rules became known as counterpoint or the practice of controlling the relationship between the different melodies.

Polyphony is one of the musical textures. Texture is how you hear the music. It may sound dense, thick, thin, or a number of different ways. Polyphony is typically described as thick or densely textured, due to the independence of multiple melodic lines.

An invention is a short composition for a keyboard instrument using two-part **counterpoint**. In a two-part invention, there are two lines of music that interweave with one another. As a result, two part inventions are **polyphonic**.

Inventions use techniques we have covered in past melody writing lessons. These are:

- *motives*: short melodic and rhythmic ideas used to create a melody
- *imitation*: the technique of repeating a musical idea (motive) in another voice or part.
- *sequence*: the repetition of a motive or phrase at a higher or lower pitch.

Below are the opening four measures of J.S. Bach's Two-Part Invention in C major, BWV 772. BWV is a numbering system used to identify Bach's compositions. This invention is based on a seven note motive found in m.1. Imitation of the opening motive can be found in the bass clef in m.1. A sequence moving downward can be found in mm.3 and 4.

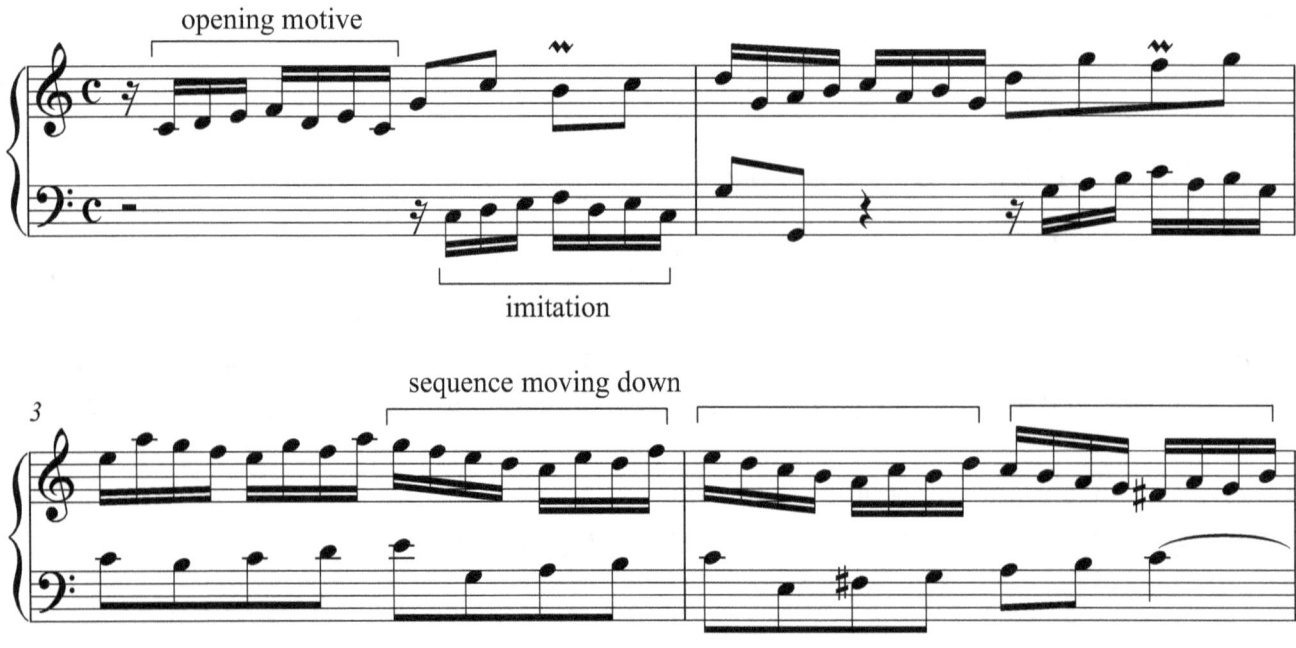

Brandenburg Concerto No. 5 - Johann Sebastian Bach

The six Brandenburg Concerti, BWV 1046-1051, by Johann Sebastian Bach is a collection of chamber music works presented to Christian Ludwig, the Margrave of Brandenburg in 1721. Margrave is a title that used to be given to Governors of German provinces.

He assembled these six *concerti grossi* and presented them, as a type of job application, to the Margrave. A ***concerto grosso*** is a baroque work for orchestra. It usually has three movements and contains a group of solo instruments called the ***concertino*** that contrasts with the full string orchestra which is known as the ***ripieno***.

Bach's title for these works was "concertos for a variety of instruments," since each one uses a different combination of instruments. He tried to use as many different combinations of common instruments as he could. Bach never actually called them the Brandenburg Concertos. The name was given to the pieces by a biographer after his death.

The Fifth Concerto in D major for **violin, flute**, and **harpsichord** makes use of a very popular chamber music ensemble (violin, flute, and harpsichord). These three instruments are the *concertino*. Bach, himself a keyboard virtuoso, included an amazing solo harpsichord cadenza in this concerto.

The first movement of this concerto is in ***ritornello*** form. In this form, a repeated section of music, known as the ritornello alternates with different musical sections.

Below is the opening of the Brandenburg Concerto No. 5. by J.S. Bach. The score below is an *open score*. In open score, each instrument has its part written on a separate staff. Traditionally the instrument names are written in Italian and appear on the left of the score from highest to lowest. On this score, the top line is the flute, and the bottom is the harpsichord, with the string section between them.

The Classical Era (ca 1750 - 1825)

The Classical era follows the Baroque era. Music from the Classical era was composed around 1750 to 1825.

Classical music is clear, structured and balanced. Form is very important, as well as harmony and tonality—that is, the key in which a piece is written.

Classical music uses dynamic contrast to emphasize movement from the tonic to new keys and then a return to the tonic. It is often loud one moment and then soft the next. It changes volume frequently. It is different from Baroque music in that it is simpler in style, without the heavy figurations and ornamentation. It is not polyphonic, that is, there is no weaving together of different tunes like those found in Baroque music.

Classical music often has a clear tune or melody with an accompaniment. Music with a single line of melody and a harmonic accompaniment is called **homophonic music** or **homophony**.

Most classical music is **absolute music**. This means that it is written specifically for the sake of being music. There are no pictorial or literary associations. It is not supposed to depict or portray anything. It's just beautiful music!

Large forms featured in the Classical period include the solo sonata, symphony, and the concerto. This period also saw a rise in **chamber music**. Chamber music is composed for smaller groups of musicians. These groups consist of two to ten players, with one player on each part. Examples of chamber music include trios, quartets, and quintets.

The greatest composers of the classical period are:

Joseph Haydn (1732–1809).
Wolfgang Amadeus Mozart (1756–1791).
Ludwig van Beethoven (1770–1827).

The classical period ended before Beethoven died. In fact, Beethoven was the one who ended it. Beethoven's later music was so new and unique that it had to be called something completely different.

Sonata Form in the Classical Era

Sonata form reached its zenith in the Classical era at the hands of Haydn, Mozart, and Beethoven.

Sonata form consists of three main sections:

1. **The exposition**: this is the opening section of sonata form. In this section, the composer introduces themes or melodies. Often there are two contrasting themes in two contrasting keys. Contrasting key or tonality is an essential part of this form.
2. **The development**: this is the middle section, and the composer *develops* the themes stated in the exposition. This developing is often done through movement to different keys.
3. **The recapitulation**: in this section the composer returns to the main themes stated in the exposition. This section does not usually change key and remains in the tonic throughout.

Sonata form was used as the basis for movements of solo sonatas, symphonies, concertos and chamber music.

Eine Kleine Nachtmusik (1st Mvt.) Wolfgang Amadeus Mozart

Wolfgang Amadeus Mozart (1756 - 1791) was one of the most important composers of the Classical era. He composed over 600 works, including some of the worlds most famous symphonies, chamber music, operas, and choral music.

Mozart gave the name **Eine kleine Nachtmusik** to his Serenade No. 13 for strings in G major, K 525. It is one of his most popular pieces, and the opening theme is famous. It was composed in 1787.

The title Eine kleine Nachtmusik means: "A little Night Music." "Nachtmusik" was a title that was given to serenades in the 18th century.

The genre of this work is chamber music. It is composed for two violins, viola, and cello and optional double bass. It can be performed as a string quartet or by a small group of string instruments, with one added double bass.

The first movement of Eine kleine Nachtmusik is in sonata form.

The complete work consists of 4 movements.

Choose the correct answers.

a. The Baroque period occurred approximately:	☐	1600-1700	☐	1650-1725
	☐	2010-2015	☐	1600-1750
b. The following are famous Baroque composers:	☐	J.S. Bach	☐	Vivaldi
	☐	Mozart	☐	Handel
c. These elements can be used to describe Baroque music:	☐	counterpoint	☐	doctrine of affections
	☐	romantic	☐	highly ornamented
d. These are Bach's 3 main periods.	☐	Leipzig	☐	Weimar
	☐	Berlin	☐	Cöthen
e. Bach composed for the following mediums.	☐	keyboard	☐	orchestra
	☐	choir	☐	chamber music
f. How many 2 part inventions did J.S. Bach write?	☐	21	☐	15
	☐	12	☐	6
g. The 3-part inventions are also known as:	☐	sonatas	☐	sinfonias
	☐	dances	☐	fugues
h. The 2-part inventions are written for this many voices:	☐	2	☐	3
	☐	6	☐	32
i. 3 elements found in the 2-part inventions are:	☐	motives	☐	sequence
	☐	imitation	☐	monophony
j. This is the numbering system used to identify Bach's works:	☐	NRA	☐	BWV
	☐	BVW	☐	BMW

Answer the following questions.

a. Who composed Brandenburg Concerto No. 5? _____

b. What genre is this work? _____

c. What 3 instruments are featured in this work? _____

d. What is this group of instruments called? _____

e. The full string orchestra in a concerto grosso is called a

☐ ripieno ☐ concertino ☐ oratorio ☐ sequence

f. The form of the first movement of Brandenburg Concerto No. 5 is

☐ rondo ☐ ritornello ☐ sonata ☐ binary

Answer the following questions as true (T) or false (F).

a. The classical period occured around 1750 to 1825. _____

b. The 3 major composers of the classical period are Haydn, Mozart and Bach. _____

c. Music with a single melodic line and accompaniment is *homophonic*. _____

d. Most classical music is *program music*. _____

e. Sonata form consists of 3 main sections. _____

f. These sections are: the *exhibition*, the *development* and the *recapitulation*. _____

g. Eine kleine Nachtmusik is *chamber music*. _____

h. Eine kleine Nachtmusisk is written for strings. _____

i. Eine kleine Nachtmusik contains 5 movements. _____

j. The first movement of Eine kleine Nachtmusik is in *sonata form*. _____

www.ingramcontent.com/pod-product-compliance
Lightning Source LLC
Chambersburg PA
CBHW081710100526
44590CB00022B/3720